BURN-UP

OR

SPLASH

DOWN

BURN-UP
OR
SPLASH
DOWN

surviving the culture shock of re-entry

MARION KNELL

Biblica Books
from InterVarsity Press

InterVarsity Press
P.O. Box 1400, Downers Grove, IL 60515-1426
World Wide Web: www.ivpress.com
Email: email@ivpress.com

InterVarsity Press® is the book-publishing division of InterVarsity Christian Fellowship/USA®, a movement of students and faculty active on campus at hundreds of universities, colleges and schools of nursing in the United States of America, and a member movement of the International Fellowship of Evangelical Students. For information about local and regional activities, write Public Relations Dept., InterVarsity Christian Fellowship/USA, 6400 Schroeder Rd., P.O. Box 7895, Madison, WI 53707-7895, or visit the IVCF website at www.intervarsity.org.

All Scripture quotations, unless otherwise indicated, are taken from the Holy Bible, New International Version®. NIV®. Copyright © 1973, 1978, 1984 by International Bible Society. Used by permission of Zondervan. All rights reserved.

Originally published in 2007 by Authentic.

Cover design: Paul Lewis
Interior design: Angela Lewis

ISBN 978-0-8308-5617-6

InterVarsity Press is committed to protecting the environment and to the responsible use of natural resources. As a member of Green Press Initiative we use recycled paper whenever possible. To learn more about the Green Press Initiative, visit www.greenpressinitiative.org.

Library of Congress Cataloging-in-Publication Data is available through the Library of Congress.

P	19	18	17	16	15	14	13	12	11	10	9	8	7	6	5	4	3	2	1
Y	29	28	27	26	25	24	23	22	21	20	19	18	17	16	15	14	13			

CONTENTS

PART I: GLOBAL NOMADS: SURVIVING THE BURN

Introduction   **3**

1. Re-Entry: What Is It?   **7**

Reverse Culture Shock   9
Change and Transition   11
Variables of Re-Entry   15

2. Re-Entry Stress   **19**

Sources of Stress   21
Signs of Cultural Stress   22
Coping with Re-Entry Stress   30

3. Preparing to Re-enter   **35**

Educating Yourself and Others   36
Saying Goodbye   38
Knowing Yourself   40
Having Realistic Expectations   42
Evaluating the Experience   43

4. Relocating   **47**

Identity   47
Employment   48
Finances   52
Housing   53
Family Needs   55
Social Skills   57
Spiritual Needs   59

5. Debriefing   63

Definition of Debriefing   64
The Use of Debriefing   66
How to Debrief   67
The Power of Debriefing   69
Children and Debriefing   70
How to Follow Up   72
Judging the Benefits   74

PART II: THIRD CULTURE KIDS: CATCHING THE WAVES

Introduction   77

6. Who Am I?   81

Definition of Third Culture Kid   82
Benefits of the TCK Experience   85
Challenges of the TCK Experience   86
Discovering Yourself   88
Putting Your Life Back Together   90
Making Choices   93

7. The Emotional Roller Coaster   95

Revisiting the Past   97
Processing Emotions   101

8. Nuts and Bolts   111

How to Fit In   112
Finances, Feasts, and phones   115
Learning the Language   120
Choosing the Right School   123
Stamping Out Worry   129
Helpful TCK Websites   132

9. The Third Culture Community   **133**

    Citizens of the World   135
    Bridging the Gap   137
    The Voyage of Self-discovery   139
    Questions and Answers   141

PART III: ON THE RECEIVING END

Introduction   **147**

10. The Reception Committee   **149**

    A Warm Welcome   150
    A Good Listener   151
    Practical Knowledge   153
    Social and Cultural Illiteracy   155
    Practical Provision   157
    Financial Provision   158
    Advice from Returning Expatriates   159

11. The Pilgrim Community   **161**

    Pilgrim's Progress   164
    TCKs in the Bible   167
    The "Pedestal" Mentality   171
    Moving On   175

Notes   **181**

DEDICATION

To Siny Widmer and Arie Baak
dear friends and colleagues who have shared my journey

ACKNOWLEDGMENTS

My thanks to Dr. Marjory Foyle and Dr. Debbie Lovell-Hawker
for their input and encouragement.

Part I

GLOBAL NOMADS: SURVIVING THE BURN

INTRODUCTION

"Houston—we have a problem." That classic understatement by Jim Lovell, commander of Apollo 13, later echoed by Tom Hanks in the film of the same name, riveted millions of viewers to their television screens. With bated breath the world waited to see if the crew would make it. And would they ever be the same again?

Using the re-entry of a spaceship as a metaphor for re-entry into one's "home" culture is not a new idea, but it does have special resonance—and not just because of the word. Making a successful splashdown requires getting the timing, the angles, the steering, and the recovery procedures just right. It took years of planning and research and the skills of over two million people to see the Apollo 11 mission successfully accomplished. Apollo 13 made it home only because all systems were shut down, other than those necessary to keep the crew alive and get them back into the earth's atmosphere.

However, many returnees would say the analogy doesn't go far enough. They don't just feel like a returning spaceship—they feel like aliens on a flying saucer from another planet! The conversation goes something like this:

"So how does it feel to be coming home?"

"What do you mean *home*?"

"How long has it taken for you to feel settled?"

"What's this word *settled*?"

"How do you feel now that you're back?"

"When does the next plane leave?"

They feel like they're floating in space, never to feel truly part of any one place, never knowing how or where to settle. And they feel as if they are totally on their own in this.

While people anticipate that going overseas will require major changes in their lifestyles and thinking, few anticipate the difficulties they will face upon return. Companies and mission agencies may run preassignment orientation programs, but not postassignment programs. This book is intended as a survival manual for those undertaking the journey. It is designed to help people plan for departure, develop coping strategies, and unpack the experience of living overseas. Because children growing up overseas have a unique experience, there's one whole section devoted to their needs.

You *can* make it back into whichever part of the earth's atmosphere you're destined for. There *are* people around who speak your language, who have survived the impact. But you need to have the heat shields in place, the life-support systems working, and a good reception committee on the other end, steering you back.

Happy landings!

> Their trajectory may be off; their thrusters may be frozen; their guidance systems may be malfunctioning; their heat shield could be cracked; their parachutes may be three blocks of ice. Clearly there are some obstacles to be overcome. (*Apollo 13*, the film)

— 1 —
RE-ENTRY: WHAT IS IT?

The following was written by someone who was evacuated in a crisis situation:

> Perhaps my experience of rapid re-entry is more common than once it was—as with re-entry from space, too rapid a descent is likely to cause more damage. There was a deep sense of being out of control and driven by circumstances, and the questions of the moral rightness of leaving when national colleagues could not. A debriefing meeting with all staff and agency representatives within ten days of return was very helpful, though the sense of disorientation

and uncertainty continued. It was only when I moved
on to new ventures that I began to feel really settled.

Is that experience confined to those who have to leave their
place of employment and residence at a moment's notice? By
no means. Even those who had plenty of advance notice of an
imminent return (six to twelve months) spoke of "frustration;"
"being stretched all the time;" "feeling confused," "disoriented,"
and "out of things."

The use of the word *re-entry* makes the assumption that this
is a return to something familiar, something you left and desire to
return to. The crew of a spaceship leaves the shores of their homeland, makes a journey into the unfamiliar territory of space, and
then re-enters the orbit of the world where they came from and
where they belong. The expatriate who has lived overseas for a
significant period of time—this can be as little as two years—may
expect to be turning the clock back, only to discover that there is
nothing familiar or repetitive in the experience. Rather, they are
entering a new world, not re-entering the old. Someone has described it this way: "We were told before we left that we would be
cloud-shaped forever. Coming from round holes going to square.
We would not fit in either world comfortably ever again. There
are no short cuts to feeling comfortable." It should be noted that
some people have no significant problems with their transition
and manage it successfully in spite of the differences.

Most employees are given some sort of cross-cultural orientation course before being sent on an overseas placement. They,
therefore, anticipate that they will be faced with major differences in customs, values, and social mores. What many fail to
realize is that upon return to what they presume will be famil-

iar—home—they will encounter culture shock similar to that which they experienced when first arriving overseas. This has been termed "reverse culture shock."

It may happen for two reasons. The first is that things have changed in their absence. Neighborhoods, currency, banking systems, and recreational pursuits all undergo regular overhauls. When you're living in a society, some changes are almost imperceptible; but, even if they are major changes, day-to-day encounters with them breed familiarity, so that they become part of the fabric of life. Moreover, the speed of change is such that you have only to be away for a short time for huge changes to take place. The acceleration of technology, in particular, drives the rate of change.

Second, the expatriates themselves have changed by virtue of living in another cultural context. And that change is likely to have gone unnoticed by them. They return home, feeling they are much the same people who went away and expecting to slot back into their place in the family and society. But not only have they changed, their friends and family have changed and moved on too. The gaps they left in people's lives have closed up and been filled by other people and other activities.

REVERSE CULTURE SHOCK

Most people going overseas are familiar with the concept of culture shock. In 1970, Philip Bock in his book *Culture Shock: A Reader in Modern Cultural Anthropology*, defined culture shock as: "Primarily an emotional reaction that follows from not being able to understand, control and predict another's behavior."[1]

John Cox, in his *Handbook for Overseas Doctors,* said: "Culture shock represents a complex gamut of feelings that may follow the abrupt change of environment after a move to a new country. Needless to say, various other factors influence this reaction. Feelings of confusion and disorientation similar to bereavement may emerge."[2] The term "reverse culture shock" indicates the re-emergence of the same culture shock symptoms on return home as were experienced on first arrival overseas. There are several reasons for its emergence.

Re-entry is a period marked by a lack of signposts, things that give meaning and shape to everyday life, such as the locality, the corner shop, the school gates, the daily routine, the places, and the people who are woven into our lives. Suddenly, everything is whipped away. And it is sudden. In the days before air travel, people had a two-month unwind period while they sailed home. Today they may get a few hours on a plane, so the change is immediate and abrupt. There is no instant cure for the loneliness, homesickness, disappointment, and grief felt at departure.

A retired, North American missionary said: "My first re-entry experience was very painful. I had been in North Africa for over four years. The decision to return for the summer came suddenly because of the 1967 war and my father's illness. I was not at all prepared for the need to readjust to life. No one had mentioned that my family, friends, church, and I would all have changed during those fifty-two months of my absence."

Reverse culture shock is also reinforced by the clash of values many people feel returning to their homeland. After some years living in a different society with different values and priorities, the expatriate subconsciously, or in some cases consciously, adopts many of these values. For those who have been in a people-intensive culture, the independence, impersonal nature, and time-conscious quality of Western society may arouse considerable antagonism. Far from embracing the culture that they left, they find themselves interrogating it, judging, and, in many cases, condemning it.

On their return from Nepal, one couple said: "We can't read the cultural signs any more. We want to stop and chat, to pass the time of day, just to have some human contact. But we need to be processed efficiently and coolly so that the next consumer can be dealt with. And if it can be done by a letter, e-mail, or phone, it will be—a personal visit is just not possible."

Reverse culture shock also sets in because *home* has been idealized and cannot possibly meet unrealistic expectations. The passage of time tends to dim our memories of the bad things and accentuate the positive. Most parents can remember how cute their babies were but tend to gloss over the sleepless nights. If the period overseas has been a particularly difficult one, the expectations tend to be higher.

CHANGE AND TRANSITION

Change as a process is external; it refers to an alteration in the environment, a different context for living. Transition is internal and it takes time.

Dr. David Pollock in *Third Culture Kids* identified the following five stages of cultural transition:[3]

1. **Involvement.** A state in which you feel you belong in a place and society; people know you; you are

committed and have meaningful relationships and
responsibilities.

2. **Leaving.** A time when you celebrate, grieve, and
   say farewells. You withdraw from responsibilities,
   commitments, and relationships. It is a stage marked
   by a mixture of emotions, such as excitement,
   anticipation, grief, and guilt.

3. **Transition.** The period when you first arrive in
   the new situation. It is best defined in the word
   chaos—feeling frustrated, confused, purposeless,
   and ignorant, not knowing people, places, and social
   skills. This can affect mental, physical, and spiritual
   health.

4. **Entering.** The moment when things begin to come
   together and make sense again, when you discover
   the route map. This is a constructive phase, when
   a new sense of control is developed, a sense of
   significance and security. At this point, a person is
   willing to experiment, to try out some of the newly
   acquired skills and experiences.

5. **Reengagement.** The point when the person feels
   secure and involved again, accepted and belonging.
   Re-adaptation has occurred, and a sense of personal
   security and identity has been reestablished.

All of this takes at least one year. We tend to want to invest
our time and energy in beginnings, but we need to tackle endings
first, to give ourselves time to acknowledge our emotions and
deal with them.

T. S. Eliot in *Little Gidding* said:[4]

> What we call the beginning is often the end
> And to make an end is to make a beginning.
> The end is where we start from.

The following is a list of questions I often use with returnees to help unpack the nature of change and their responses to it. You might like to use it for yourself if you are in a time of uprooting.

- Complete this sentence: "Change is . . ."
- Of all the changes you have been through, which one do you think you handled the best? Why?
- Complete this sentence: "The best thing about change is . . ."
- What is the toughest change in your life so far? Why?
- What is the best advice for someone in the midst of change?

Returnees came up with a wide selection of adjectives to complete the first sentence. "Change is: exciting, tiring, constant, unpredictable. . . ." The response is of course determined, in part, by the current stage of transition. Someone who has just arrived may be caught up in the honeymoon period, the time when everything is exciting and new. If it is their first taste of bacon in two years, or the thrill of hot running water, then it is a pleasurable experience. Or it may all be *so* new that they feel overwhelmed, out of control. A woman who had been abroad for four years and was on her first visit home recalled: "I was met by my family and couldn't keep my eyes open for the two-hour drive from the airport. My mother had baked a cake to celebrate, and all I could do was go to bed!"

A returnee's reaction is also shaped by previous experiences of change. A person's experience of one move will very much influence attitudes toward the next move. If the last move was a positive experience, then the anticipation for the next will be that things will be fine. A negative experience leaves people with feelings of apprehension and anxiety, anticipating and dreading the problems.

Change is a normal part of life for everyone, and this is particularly true of any transition. Stress invariably accompanies change. A certain amount of stress is good for us because it keeps our lives in tension and motivates us to meet responsibilities. Knowing our sources of stress and likely responses to them helps us cope in demanding situations. The next chapter will look more deeply at re-entry stress.

The amount of stress a person in transition feels is intensified by two things: (1) the period of time involved (the shorter the time, the more painful the experience), and (2) the differences between the point of departure and the point of completion. Apart from the rapid nature of re-entry already referred to, in most cases, there is a world of difference (often literally) between the point of departure and the point of completion.

When it comes to re-entry, we must factor in the culture a person has lived in and the degree to which the person has identified with it. The closer the identification and the more rigid the cultural mores of that society, the harder it will be to readjust to life back in the passport culture. This is particularly significant for children who have been born and brought up overseas. Their sense of identity is put under intense pressure when they return, at whatever age.

VARIABLES OF RE-ENTRY

Several variables affect the ability to cope with the stress of re-entry. The variables we will consider are timing, reasons for re-entry, economic standards, preparation and support systems, and personality traits.

Timing

A crisis evacuation is obviously loaded with a lot more anguish than a planned withdrawal for whatever reason. Rapid re-entry denies the person the opportunity to say goodbye to people and places and bring closure to the period spent abroad. It prevents adequate plans for disposing of belongings and making provision for an appropriate place of reception.

It is generally acknowledged that people withdraw from a situation six months before they actually leave. So a person needs at least six months to make preparations for departure and arrival. Given that the individual has both a life cycle and a career cycle to consider, and family life has its own cycles and seasons, deciding when to make the move becomes critical. Juggling school years with job responsibilities and deciding financial terms and replacement staff can be a harrowing task. It is hard to get it just right for everyone. The right time to move for one child may be unfortunate for another. If possible, moves should be made at the best time for the one who least likes change.

Reasons for Re-Entry

Many folk ostensibly come home for their children's education. I say *ostensibly* because children's education is often given as the acceptable reason for quitting a post that is not suitable for other reasons, such as location, team dynamics, and social incompatibility.

Another reason for re-entry can be retirement. In this case, the person is not only giving up home and friends but also, for many, their identity as well. This is reinforced by Western society, which begins by asking a new acquaintance, "What's your name?" and follows it up with, "What do you do?" Our identities are vested in our social roles and, for many, the absence of a role creates a confusion of identity. After thirty years overseas, one returnee reflected: "I was sad at leaving my friends who were loved and relationships and situations that were part of my life. I was perplexed at my new identity and what I was supposed to be doing, a sort of detachment and inertia, a feeling of uselessness, some fear at suddenly realizing I was getting old and that life had taken a major turn."

Some choose re-entry and some have re-entry forced on them: the firm decides their services are needed elsewhere; a national is promoted to take over an operation; funding for a project is withdrawn; or the death of the wage earner means the rest of the family can no longer stay. In such cases, there is sometimes a sense of being a victim and needing to find someone to blame. This immediately sets the stage for conflict upon re-entry. The desirability of the change colors the perception and the attitude toward the process.

Economic Standards

The difference in the standard of living between the place left and the place of arrival can also be enormous. Areas of the world where it is normal to have a live-in maid at very little cost are a world away from suburban Europe or the United States where the cost of housing is sky-high and help, if it can be found, is exceedingly expensive.

Similarly, the expatriate worker can find himself or herself moving from being a big fish in a little pond to being a little fish in a big pond. This can affect self-esteem and coping strategies as well as the ability to take on new responsibilities.

Preparation and Support Systems

The degree to which someone is prepared or has the opportunity to do preparation before returning can immensely improve the process. Similarly, the situation to which someone is returning will obviously help or hinder. When war erupted in her country of service and she had to leave immediately, one nurse wrote: "I was returning home to nothing and to no one. Everything I owned had been stolen."

Two things play significant roles in a returnee's readjustment: how much he or she has answered the "What next?" question and how much help is available in navigating the course.

Personality Traits

Finally, and not least, a person's disposition shapes his or her attitude toward change, feelings toward what awaits, and tolerance levels toward strange and sometimes unacceptable behavior. "Know yourself" is a helpful adage when it comes to coping with change and transition.

> We do not see things as they are; we see things as we are. (Talmud)[5]

> We have a main bus B undervolt. . . . We've got a lot of thruster activity here. . . . We just went off-line. . . . There's another master alarm here. . . . We've got multiple caution warnings. . . . We've got a computer restart. (*Apollo 13*, the film)

— 2 —

RE-ENTRY STRESS

Kalvero Oberg identified cultural stress as "the anxiety that results from losing all our familiar signs and symbols of social intercourse."[1] The British psychiatrist, Dr. Marjory Foyle speaks of the "discontinuity of social relationship."[2] This is the loss of all that is familiar to us—that which makes sense of our lives and gives life structure and purpose.

The words most commonly used by people describing their feelings on re-entry are *loss*, *grief*, *bereavement*, *depression*, and *loneliness*. In composing the questionnaires for my research on this subject, I made the mistake of asking the question, "What was your biggest joy upon return?" I discovered that the word *joy* was too emotionally loaded, and I received these responses:

- "There was nothing joyful about it."
- "There was no joy because of why I had to return."
- "Caring for mum—it wasn't joy. It wasn't home. I hated it."
- "No idea—it wasn't joyful. The chance to do something new?"

Such a question tended to elicit negative responses; whereas, a question like, "What was the best part about coming back?" encouraged people to look for something good in all the upheaval. The responses to this question were more positive:

- "Getting reconnected with family."
- "Twenty-four-hour electricity and hot running water."
- "Catching up with friends."
- "Anonymity."

One of the greatest problems people face on re-entry is that they believe they are alone in feeling like this, that there must be something wrong with them. Consequently, they often hide their feelings and retreat into *themselves*, thus actually impairing their ability to make an effective new start. The best preparation for coming home is to be aware of the transition and the likely effects.

Normalizing the experience is a key to handling re-entry successfully; it is crucial not to criticize yourself or feel guilty for your reactions. If you can accept your feelings as normal, then the readjustment process will be smoother and possibly shorter. Later, we will look at practical ways to prepare for departure and re-entry, but, I first want to define some general sources of stress. Then, we will focus on signs of cultural stress and discuss its emotional effects and different ways of reacting to it.

SOURCES OF STRESS

We confront many sources of stress in our daily lives. The following is a list of the major types of stress along with a brief definition:

- **Psychological.** Loss of self-esteem due to changes; loss of identity; or emotional instability because of grief, loneliness, or fear of the future.

- **Physical.** Tiredness leading up to departure; differences in climate; inadequacy of appropriate clothing; age upon arrival.

- **Family Tensions.** Children reacting to return by becoming clingy; parents unable to sustain their own and their children's emotional needs; lack of privacy; lack of a home base or inadequacy of accommodation; the difficulty of finding a job; the place of relocation.

- **Support Systems.** The availability of resources (financial, technical, and personal) to help returnees through the period of adjustment in the absence of people who understand the experience.

- **Occupational.** Being unemployed; job-hunting; lack of appropriate skills; recognition of validity of previous employment.

- **Historical.** Past struggles that are unresolved; traumatic evacuation; poor relationships; rejection; lack of involvement in decision-making; frustrations with bureaucracy, political events, or management decisions.

- **Cultural.** Unfamiliarity with the receiving culture; false assumptions on the part of the returnees and those receiving them; incomplete knowledge of family history and having no part in it; inability of family to readjust totally to the returnee; unmet needs due to false expectations; hostility to the new culture.

SIGNS OF CULTURAL STRESS

There are several signs of cultural stress that we will cover in this section. The most common symptoms are alienation, grief, frustration, loss, exhaustion, anger, and confusion.

Alienation

One returnee put it this way: "People said, 'It must be so nice to be home,' when I hadn't really thought where home is."

Another said: "We look out of our window or drive around these suburbs and see the never-ending houses with their neat little gardens and the cars parked outside, which are all a little different, but to us all somehow merge into one. We could be anywhere, and while everyone else is connected to this world, it is going to take some time for us to adjust."

On return, it is not just that everything is different and strange, but rather that it makes *you* feel the stranger, the alien. People are doing and saying things you don't understand, even though you speak the same language and have the same passport. The values they hold, their goals, and their perspectives on life are a world away from what you are used to. You find yourself increasingly frustrated with people and with the way things work (or don't work) and critical of a culture you once embraced, if not enthusiastically, at least comfortably. Your ignorance of acceptable behavior, transport systems, and social mores make the local people seem positively hostile as they greet your innocent remarks and questions with blank looks or unfriendly glares.

In response to the question, "What was your biggest frustration?" typical replies included:

- "Being unaccepted in society and coping with different attitudes"
- "Failure of folk to understand what we'd left and no idea of what to do with us"
- "People not understanding or not interested enough to try and understand"

The hardest thing is not just that no one understands you, but that few are really interested in where you've been or what you've been doing. The odd, superficial questions, "Where have you been all this time?" and "Was it hot?" are not really invitations to delve into your bottomless pit of outrageous stories from *over there*. The interest wanes fairly quickly once you embark on a detailed description of a life outside the parameters of their experience and that has little relevance to what they'll be doing tomorrow or the day after.

Grief

Without exception, even after a difficult assignment, grief is the overriding emotion dominating the returnee. Leaving a place and people with whom your life has become inextricably linked is a bereavement. The fact that they are on the other side of the world and, therefore, cannot be visited at the drop of a hat makes it even more difficult. For some returnees going back will never be possible, either because of a political situation or because they lack the funds to make the trip. Any loss is a form of bereavement, but the experience of re-entry is an acute form.

It is not helpful when the people to whom you are returning assume that you are delighted to be back. They think this is what you've been waiting for with bated breath all these years. After escaping from a war situation, one woman commented:

"People asked, 'You'll be glad to be home safely?' I wasn't glad, and I didn't feel as if I was home!"

To them, you are returning home; for you, particularly for children, you are leaving home. Those re-entering often find it hard to grieve, and many are denied the space, time, and companions they need to process the grief they feel. But, as in any bereavement, the process of mourning can only be navigated successfully if it is given all of those outlets. Denial of grief and suppression of its expression does not make it go away. It is pushed to the bottom, only to resurface at a later date under another pretext or another trigger and may be much harder to handle. Worse, a withdrawal into one's self, a denial of the feeling, can lead to escapism of various kinds, including alcoholism, tranquilizers, and suicidal thoughts.

Frustration

Frustration is part of the alienation process. People come back with specific skills that are no longer appropriate and that they can no longer put to use. The jobs for which they feel qualified are sometimes not open to them because their time overseas has not been seen as a positive step on their career ladder. Much frustration is due to ignorance about travel, shopping, moving, and registering with appropriate authorities. An expatriate who had spent several years in Southeast Asia recalled: "At Victoria Coach Station, needing to phone home to say when I'd arrive, I didn't know the new phone box system or recognize the new coins, so I had to ask help from the person waiting in the queue behind me. She was dark-skinned, wearing a sari and answered in a Yorkshire accent: 'Oh yes, dear, I'll help yer—it must be 'ard when yer've jus cum from abroad!'"

Many people do not realize how closely they have identified with the local culture and, therefore, how much they have adopted that way of behaving, those values, and those expectations. With an embarrassed grin, an expatriate in his early forties narrated the following incident: "My wife went shopping for shoes and found the prices outrageously high. So she told this to the shopkeeper and wanted to bargain as we always did in Thailand. The shopkeeper was embarrassed and angry. Her mother took her by the hand and quickly left the shop."

Loss

Loss is not felt just in the sense of bereavement or personal dissociation. Loss also relates to status and identity. Over there you were known as the person who was in charge of _____, who lived at _____, who ran the _____. Back home you are a nobody; you have no defining status at work, socially, and sometimes in the family. While people are away, the roles they filled before have been taken over by others, and the gaps they left in the fabric of society and family have been filled. Life goes on when you are not there, and your return is something of a shock and a resurrection. It's as if you have come back from the dead; no one quite knows where to put you.

When the economic diversity is great between the place you left and that to which you are returning, there can be considerable loss of status, which also disrupts the family pattern of living. In areas where it is the norm to have a live-in maid, maybe even a chauffeur, gardener, and handyman, and where homes come with a large swimming pool and grounds, it can be a come-down to return to a large city where house prices are astronomical and help is so rare and expensive that the family has to rely on its own resources.

Exhaustion

Change of any kind is tiring, and cultural change is doubly so. Feeling tired, not sleeping well, having headaches and problems with the digestive system can all be symptoms of re-entry stress. People arrive home tired after the whirlwind of packing up and closing down. They have had little time for adjustment—it's off to the airport, on to the plane, and off into the New (or Old) World. And it isn't just that you arrive tired; you immediately have to embark on a busy schedule. There is the process of setting up house, finding a job, settling children into schools, and finding your way around the neighborhood. Even if you're returning to the place you left, chances are it will have undergone major changes. Making new friends and dealing with bureaucracy is all extremely exhausting. There's no reason to feel strange or guilty for feeling tired and in need of a vacation. In fact, a vacation might just be the best thing.

Anger

You feel anger toward yourself, toward the people around you, or toward the systems that conspire to defeat you and thwart your every attempt to settle. You can find yourself enraged at the materialism that surrounds you and at the pettiness of people's values. A middle-aged Scotsman returning to middle England from the continent remarked:

> I find people petty (in general) and their mindset I do
> not understand. It is so concerned about appearances
> and not about people and their needs. I find this area
> very unreal where people are concerned that some-
> one puts up a fence that ruins the appearance of their
> neighborhood. To me it looks all right and is built by
> a professional fence-builder. The fence is to protect
> a Down's syndrome child from harassment by local

children. People write to the local paper to condemn the father who built the fence but no one writes to stick up for the child. Please forgive my tirade; I get hot under the collar!

Anger is often a way of dealing with grief; it cloaks the true feelings. It is easier to be angry than to deal with grief. In fact, anger is a good way to disguise any sort of pain. It keeps people away and prevents having to disclose true feelings. In her autobiography, *Still Talking*, Joan Rivers described anger as "a symptom, a way of cloaking and expressing feelings too awful to experience directly—hurt, bitterness, grief and, most of all, fear."[3]

In the case of crisis evacuation, anger can be another way of expressing guilt—the guilt of leaving behind national colleagues who had no choice but to stay and face whatever was coming.

Confusion

The re-entering stage is marked by chaos and confusion, not knowing where anything belongs, least of all yourself. The confusion is due to the lack of signposts mentioned earlier. You are living in a maze, and there are no signs to the center. You may seem to be going round and round, achieving less and less, and feeling more and more disoriented. Confusion is enhanced because you *expected* to know the ropes, to feel as if you belonged—this is my country, and I'm the stranger! Disappointed expectations are a major cause of re-entry stress.

Language is part of this confusion because words change meaning. Someone giggles when you innocently use a word that was current when you were last here but now has a double meaning. Words sometimes come to mean the opposite of what they originally meant. For example, after the film *Wayne's World*, the word *wicked* came to mean "excellent."

This is intensified if you are used to working in a second language. A friend of mine, returning after years in Algeria, experienced acute embarrassment when buying a railway ticket. This is her story:

> I walked up to the ticket office and said quite clearly
> (so I thought), "A return ticket to London, please."
> Seeing the blank look on the face of the booking
> clerk, I repeated my request a little more slowly. At
> the third attempt, it dawned on me that I was speaking not in English but in French. Unwilling to admit
> my mistake and appear a complete fool, I said very
> slowly and in heavily accented English, "A go-come-
> ticket to London, please" and duly received what I
> needed. A week later I returned to the station in order
> to make the same journey. I strolled up to the ticket
> office and said in bright, perfect English, "A return
> ticket to London please." "My goodness!" replied the
> same booking clerk. "Your English has improved in
> a week!"

Disorientation can result in physical symptoms such as tiredness, tearfulness, or irritability, as well as an overall numbness and inability to make decisions. And this happens at just the time when major decisions have to be made. If possible, it is advisable to create temporary structures to support your life and postpone major decisions until you are in a better state of mind to make them.

Knowing your own reactions to stressful situations is particularly helpful when identifying re-entry stress. The symptoms I mentioned above are commonly identified by people returning to base. But all of us have our own characteristic stress symptoms or ways we know we are likely to respond when placed under strain. Recognizing those symptoms helps us to identify the causes and deal with the consequences. It is particularly helpful if a family can spend time looking at their individual traits so that they can make allowances for each other and bear with the reactions engendered by the transition.

Parents need to be especially sensitive to the needs and personalities of younger children, who may not have the vocabulary to articulate their feelings, but whose behavior patterns may change radically as an expression of the stress they feel. For all of us there are physical manifestations of stress as well as emotional ones. When I am under stress, I am likely to take it out on a piano if there is one in the vicinity. It may not sound pretty to anyone who happens to be within earshot, but it sure makes me feel better!

COPING WITH RE-ENTRY STRESS

To successfully cope with re-entry stress, individuals must accept the process, learn to communicate effectively, and set realistic goals.

Acceptance

The first step in coping with the stress of re-entry is to acknowledge it is normal and accept it is a phase of life you have to go through. It is a process, and it *will* pass. There will be pain, and this needs to be anticipated and managed. Acceptance leads to a healthy resolution of the re-entry experience.

Unhealthy coping strategies include the following:

- **Denial.** Ignoring unpleasant circumstances or feelings; joking about the way things are, but not acknowledging the hostility one feels. This only offers temporary relief.

- **Suppression.** Pushing feelings down into the subconscious where they remain buried until triggered by a later event.

- **Withdrawal.** Finding forms of escapism that enable you to avoid the reality of the situation. Staying indoors, refusing to interact with the environment, or finding excuses for not meeting people are common behavior patterns at this stage.

- **Rationalization.** Finding plausible reasons for feeling the way you do without treating the root causes.

Acceptance also means acknowledging that while things are different, they are not necessarily worse. Exactly the same sort of allowances had to be made when first arriving overseas in the new culture.

Communication

It is important to find someone you can talk to frankly and who has the time to listen and the ability to empathize with your feelings. Those who have not been through the experience will not fully understand what you are going through, but, in the absence of such a person, a sympathetic listener goes a long way.

Most of those back home will have a limited concentration span when it comes to hearing your overseas experiences. They are not really bored; they just have difficulty relating to it. It is often a good idea to first give people only a taste of your experiences, and then tell them more as they request it.

Communication is also about educating people who will be part of your future life on the dynamics of your situation. This is particularly important for the extended family, and I will discuss more of this when dealing with preparation for return.

Realistic Goals

"Rome wasn't built in a day," goes the old adage. When going through the re-entry process, it is important to set realistic goals in all areas for yourself and for your family. Job prospects, housing possibilities, school standards, and social integration all take time to investigate and integrate. In his book, *A Place for You*, Paul Tournier says:[4]

> We must always be letting go what we have
> acquired, and acquiring what we do not possess,
> leaving one place in order to find another, abandon-
> ing one support in order to reach another, turning our

backs on the past to thrust wholeheartedly towards
the future.

> We're gonna have to turn everything off, or they're not going to make it through re-entry. (*Apollo 13*, the film)

—3—

PREPARING TO RE-ENTER

In an ideal world, returning expatriates have at least six months notice of their intended date of departure. That means time to pack up belongings, arrange transportation, say goodbye to friends, and hand over responsibilities at one end. At the other, it means time to choose somewhere to live, apply for jobs (this is becoming easier with online applications), get the children into schools, and begin to adjust perspectives for starting afresh with positive attitudes.

Most of us, however, do not live in an ideal world. Even in cases where there is adequate notice of relocation, the real situation may be that, in the meantime, responsibilities are not reduced. There may be tasks to be finished and less time to do them in, and emotional attachments make it difficult to let go and embrace the new. The very act of daily living in certain situations, whether because of climate, political tensions, or health risks, is so energy-sapping that there is nothing left in the reserve tanks to begin the relocation process.

Apollo 13 made it home because the astronauts used all the power in the LEM batteries and life-support systems that were intended for use on the moon. These were auxiliary systems brought into use as energy to replace the normal systems. Does the analogy have anything to add to the re-entry scenario? Where is the auxiliary power going to come from? Who is going to assist you through your re-entry?

EDUCATING YOURSELF AND OTHERS

One of the first steps in preparing to re-enter is to tell it how it is. That means having information for yourself about the process, as described in chapters 1 and 2, and disseminating that information to the people who need to know and can help you through it. That list includes your immediate family, that is, your spouse and children, who are most affected by the move. Each person will be affected differently by the move, depending on where it comes in their lifecycles, how much say they had in the decision, and their degrees of attachment to the current location.

It is important that parents take special care to listen to their children before departure, to reorient them in a realistic way, bearing in mind that many of them have never lived in the land of your passport. Much has been written on the subject of Third Culture Kids (TCKs), their characteristics, and the challenges the TCK lifestyle brings. For them to approach the new beginning with confidence, they need to unpack their life experiences so far and have some pointers as to how to handle the future. This move will be a major change for them. School will be very different, and so may sports, hobbies, language, clothes, eating habits, and food. What is expected of them may be widely divergent from what has been the norm, and they need to be prepared for that. They need to be prepared to adjust their thinking and behavior where appropriate and also to retain a sense of personal identity and integrity. They should know they do not have to compromise their values and principles in order to fit in. There are several ways to prepare TCKs and to set up support systems for them, and these will be addressed in Part II of this book.

Next, your extended family, which longs to see you home but feels a little helpless and inadequate to deal with you—this alien being—needs some direction and guidance regarding your needs and feelings. Someone who has never lived overseas will find it difficult to step into the shoes of those re-entering and see things from their perspectives or feel the emotions they experience. They will not be aware of your unfamiliarity with the surroundings and culture because they assume you are coming *home*.

This is when it is good to keep in regular contact by letters or e-mail and be quite frank about what is going on in your life. For your own well-being, it's helpful to keep some sort of journal to chart your feelings and how you deal with them. Journaling also helps you acknowledge those feelings. Whether you, at any stage, want to open that up to other members of the family is up to you. In some cases, it may be easier than having to say the same things over and over.

The other people who need to be educated are the "official welcomers," including the firm or agency you have been working for, your colleagues, your wider circle of friends, your home church, supporters, and interested parties. Some of these may have shared your experiences, in which case they will know how to help. Others may be ignorant of the issues involved. For instance, some firms do not always provide the right advice on reapplying for jobs or composing a resume appropriate to the current home market that reflects the benefit of your service overseas. Some in this wider group may have professional skills that would be useful with the practical details of relocation, such as signing up with government agencies, setting up bank accounts and insurance policies, and dealing with public utilities. But your friends can't help if they don't know what is needed.

A book such as the one you are reading now will help these groups understand the dynamics of the process. There is even a chapter especially for them! Sometimes it helps for the information to come from an objective outsider and for them to realize that there are issues and concerns common to all who share the experience of re-entry. It takes the returnee out of the "special case" category.

SAYING GOODBYE

Closure means the whole act of saying goodbye and drawing relationships and responsibilities to a close. Bringing good closure to a period in your life enables you to make a good beginning in the new place. It also helps you build on past experiences and learn from them. Good closure also helps you find something positive in what may have been a negative experience.

The process of closure also assists in coming to terms with the reasons for moving. If you take time to plan your departure in emotional as well as practical terms, you have the opportunity to bring some objectivity to what is subjectively a very emotional experience. There may be some disappointment or bitterness at the end of an assignment. You may be disappointed because the move didn't quite work out the way you thought it would: it didn't live up to your expectations; or you feel you have been badly treated by those who employed you, who withdrew before the task was completed or did not give enough notice or support.

Unresolved anger and bitterness are carried forward into a new situation if they have not been dealt with. Problems are seldom left fully behind; we merely export them to our new location. This means it is important to resolve conflicts before leaving, even if you will never again live in the same place or work with those individuals. Having things out in the open and setting the record straight also facilitate dealing with any guilt from those you are leaving behind. As mentioned earlier, it is usually in the event of evacuation that this is felt most keenly and where there is little or no opportunity to deal with it.

In his book *Third Culture Kids*, Dr. David Pollock uses the helpful acronym RAFT as a way of dealing with goodbyes:[1]

- **Reconciliation.** Putting relationships right.

- **Affirmation.** Saying what was good about the experience; it prevents leaving from becoming a funeral.

- **Farewell.** Saying goodbye to people, places, and pets in culturally appropriate ways.

- **Think Destination.** Think realistically about what awaits you at the other end.

While speaking at a seminar on transition, I was discussing the need to say goodbye and, after a while, noticed a lady in the front row with tears streaming down her face. "We left in such a hurry. I never had the chance to say goodbye, and it still really hurts." She later told me her re-entry, due to an emergency health crisis in the family, had occurred nine years before.

Many people have reflected on the benefit of returning once more to get a sense of closure. One person who had been overseas for only two years said: "In some ways I did not feel settled again until I revisited Nepal six years later!"

Another, who struggled with re-entry after a crisis evacuation, advised: "Take time to sort out all your feelings about returning, especially if you have returned earlier than envisaged and under difficult circumstances. If necessary, return at some stage to say all the goodbyes you weren't able to say the first time."

KNOWING YOURSELF

I have already remarked that returnees do not anticipate the changes that have taken place in their absence. Foremost among these are the changes in themselves. Here is a checklist for change:

- **How have you changed *socially*?** What are your foremost values? How much of the culture around you have you adopted, maybe without even realizing it? How much are the values of this culture in conflict with those of your home culture? For instance, attitudes toward family, the importance of people and relationships, and attitudes toward material possessions will probably have shaped your thinking and behavior.

- **How much have your circumstances changed** *economically*? This can be particularly important if you have been living somewhere where labor is cheap and your money goes a long way. You may have become used to all sorts of perks that you no longer regard as luxuries.

- **How much have you changed** *emotionally*? In part, this will depend on how much your value system has changed during your time abroad. But it may also be that you had less in the way of emotional support systems and, consequently, became more independent and emotionally resilient. If you have been living in a two-thirds world community and have seen a lot of hardship, deprivation, and suffering, you may be more sensitive and easily hurt. You may also be angry at the injustices you have witnessed.

- **How much have you changed** *physically*? Sometimes change is as little as growing a beard because that is the cultural norm. Sometimes the diet has led to a healthy weight loss. Food preferences may have changed as a result of being exposed to a different way of eating. This can be quite disconcerting for your family members who prepared all your favorite foods to welcome you back, only to discover that these foods are not at all to your liking any more. Illness may be one of the reasons for leaving, which will impact your reserves to deal with the upcoming change and may also shock those you are returning to.

- **How much have you changed** *politically*? Being on the world stage removes the cultural blinders that cause us to see everything through our own nation's best interests. Being on the receiving end of globalization may produce a very different attitude toward multinational corporations, the workings of the United Nations, and the justice of others' causes. Many expatriates return with a rather radical political stance and agenda and find themselves marginalized as a result.

HAVING REALISTIC EXPECTATIONS

Having realistic expectations comes under the "Think Destination" heading of the RAFT diagram. Many people plan their return wearing a pair of rose-tinted glasses. They remember all that was good and pleasant about the place they left behind and fail to factor in the deceitfulness of memory or the changes that will inevitably have taken place to all that they trust and hold dear. One of the tough things about relocating is the unpredictability of it all. That is something you expect when you go overseas, but you anticipate being able to read the signs correctly when you return—and that's not how it works.

Those who cope best are people who have maintained good links while overseas. Personal links are established by way of regular communication, visits, sending photos, and keeping family and friends up to date on your personal situation and being interested in theirs. Cultural links are forged by getting newspapers and magazines, watching television, or surfing educational websites that give you the current state of affairs.

The important thing is to anticipate what the likely flashpoints will be on your return. The following questions can prove invaluable in doing so:

- Do you have a job to go to? If not, how difficult will it be to get one?

- What will be your children's emotional and practical needs?

- What resources, especially financial, will you have?

- Will you re-enter the same community, or are you starting all over again?

- What added responsibilities will you have (for example, aging parents)?

- Will you be on your own in this? If you have a partner, will he or she be around or traveling?

EVALUATING THE EXPERIENCE

In some ways evaluation is an ongoing process, looked at slightly differently depending on where you are on the journey of return. Unless you have been signed up for a proper debriefing program (see chapter 5), you may not have the opportunity to unpack your experiences satisfactorily. Sometimes it is helpful to take time out between packing up and arriving home. One woman from Southeast Asia with her three children remarked: "The cheapest flight home started in the opposite direction, toward a tropical island that enabled us to have a good holiday in a different climate and culture."

Such serendipity is rare and usually has to be planned. A halfway point, culturally and emotionally, can be a good place to take a step back and evaluate what has been going on in your life and the lives of those around you over the years of the last assignment. Another family I know deliberately booked themselves into accommodations in Cyprus for two weeks before returning to the United Kingdom from a job in Pakistan. They arrived home in a much more relaxed frame of mind, with renewed supplies of energy and a better idea of what the next stage would be for them.

When preparing this book, I surveyed a wide range of people who had been through the re-entry experience. The following advice comes from them:

- Take time to prepare—it *is* tough but you *will* make it.
- Plan a proper departure—good endings make for good beginnings.
- Make sure to prepare those waiting for you to return.
- Don't verbalize negatively in front of the children.
- Don't let anger dictate your behavior.
- Accept systems designed for those who belong.

- Plan your return on-field.

- Ensure that you have a support network.

- Take a halfway break.

- Explore how to get back into the job market.

- Rebuild relationships.

- Expect it to be a transition—be ready for it.

- Remember your first time overseas—this experience will mirror it.

> We can't use the computer. What do we do for orientation? (*Apollo 13*, the film)

— 4 —

RELOCATING

The crew of Apollo 13 found that the only way to navigate was by fixing their sights on the one steady point of reference—the earth. They lined up the spacecraft with the earth in the center of their window and made the appropriate course corrections. When relocating, it helps to have some fixed points of reference as a starting place. This chapter focuses on the main areas that can provide starting points. Following up on some of the issues raised in the last chapter, we will examine both what can be done to focus on those points before leaving and what needs to be done after arrival.

IDENTITY

Having lived in the south of France for all his married life, a British computer engineer returning with his teenage daughters said: "One of our biggest frustrations was being considered of no fixed abode by banks and anyone seeking credit ratings. The

Royal Bank of Scotland was the only group who would take our French bank statements and offer a mortgage on the basis of them. It has taken a year before people start to consider us as anything other than fly-by-nights."

A single lady who spent thirty years in various parts of North Africa and the Middle East as a radiographer complained: "At the age of fifty-four, I couldn't prove my identity when I tried to hire a video from Blockbuster!"

Bureaucracy is famous for removing you from the national systems once you've left but notorious for being difficult about admitting you back in. If you live in one of those parts of the world where you have to have an identity card, you are marginally better off. But in many areas you still need a credible life history and proof of dependability when it comes to getting loans as well as demonstrating your right to grants, healthcare, social assistance, and education.

Many people do, of course, retain a bank account in their country of passport and some still own property. Even if you're not going to have a large amount of money passing through your account, it helps to retain the link. For many, it is more advantageous not to have money back home while overseas because of the tax benefits of being offshore. Whichever route you choose, preliminary inquiries need to be set up before you return home, if not by you, then by someone acting on your behalf.

EMPLOYMENT

Unless you are relocating with the same company, finding a job can be a nightmare. Even with the same company, you need to assume you will have to rebuild working relationships. It is important to be *au fait* with the current workings of the home office as well as the concerns and interests of those employed there. It is all too easy to slip into the habit of constantly referring to life overseas and activities and interests that have little in common with your colleagues. Even within the same company, systems change. Procedures and practices are constantly under review, especially if a firm is downsizing. Often there are accommodations with regard to working from home, flexible hours, and desk sharing within an office.

If you are returning to find a new job, then it is vital to update your portfolio so that it reflects all your relevant proficiencies. Returning expatriates need to carefully document their experiences, accomplishments, languages, qualifications, and training acquired during their stay in the host country. These can be accompanied by photos, newspaper clippings, and details of those with whom and for whom you worked. Because you may be considered unusual, a fairly full record cataloguing the benefits and skills gained from living overseas is needed. You may then be seen as someone with something special to offer rather than someone unable to fit in.

Most people continue to subscribe to a professional journal while overseas to keep up to speed with developments. It may also be necessary to investigate the avenues of retraining or refresher courses when you return. Several people surveyed commented on retraining, either because it had been forced on them or because they had discovered the benefits for themselves. One returnee who had been a headmistress in a West African school remarked: "There was a shortage of primary teachers in Manchester so I was welcomed—to teach immigrant West Indians!"

Another, who spent some years in Zimbabwe, said: "I am a U.K.-qualified nurse, midwife, and health visitor, and I have a master's degree. Upon reapplying to the National Health Service, I soon realized I was on a steep learning curve when I discovered that even the names given to my qualifications had changed! However, I could sign up for a four-month refresher course in a post that was less demanding than my overseas career."

It is also important to be flexible and prepared to try something different, maybe even to settle for less seniority, just to get your feet on the ladder. Being in a less stressful and demanding job can give you more time to adjust to life back home as well as to look around for a position you really want.

After working with a nongovernmental organization in a particularly stressful refugee situation, a middle-aged lady reflected: "I wanted to do something practical and less stressful for a while so I got a job cooking and cleaning at an Outdoor Activity Center, which was a really refreshing experience. After a year, when I applied for a professional job, I did not find that my time overseas was seen as beneficial to my career but more as a career break. I was not familiar with all the up-to-date jargon in the healthcare world, and I think this counted against me. However, I was the only applicant for the job, and they took me on temporarily. I don't think they have any regrets. I am now on permanent contract."

Sometimes timing, circumstances, and the needs of the family dictate that you settle somewhere soon and earn enough money to get by. At that stage, ingenuity and flexibility can work to your advantage. A doctor with three children ages ten, twelve, and fourteen, who returned after eight years in Thailand with her husband, also a doctor, reported: "As I began doing anesthetic sessions, I realized some of my expertise, though fine in Asia, was inappropriate for the United Kingdom. I retrained as a General Practitioner. The GP we signed on with needed a trainee and then the practice wanted a female partner who had had her family. So it all fell into place."

Even voluntary work undertaken overseas can add to your resume. It shows future employers you are someone who wants to get involved; it tells them you are a caring person and can network with people of varying abilities and backgrounds.

As well as creating a good resumé of your career, backed up with appropriate documentation, you may need to brush up on your interviewing skills. Senior management in your present company may help you with this, or you might take advantage of one of the many consulting agencies and arrange a session. But this will cost you. Better still, find a friend at home whose job involves interviewing people and get a free how-to-do-it session.

Job hunting takes time and networking skills. If you build it into your predeparture plans, arrange for people back home to do some of the work for you by finding opportunities and keeping you informed of the state of the market. The growth of the Internet has made job hunting from a distance much easier, with many firms taking applications only online.

If there are children coming back, then it may be advisable for only one of the parents to take employment initially, at least the sort of employment that demands strict adherence to hours. Several able career women have said to me that if they could do it over again, they would not rush into employment but would get the family settled first. And for them, getting the family settled meant getting themselves settled regarding home, services, and neighborhood. When they felt at peace, the rest of the family settled more quickly. For some, this meant waiting to take a job; for others, it meant working minimal hours or doing voluntary work to keep their skills up. One doctor-mom commented: "The tensions were that we needed to work, especially my husband. I didn't do much until we had been back for over a year, but we also needed to spend time with the kids."

FINANCES

Besides employment, one of the greatest challenges facing returnees is money—or the lack of it. There may be an immediate shortfall between leaving one job and finding another. There may be a longer-term shortfall because the tax-free salary and allowances are no longer available. Everything costs more, and there are a lot more things you are expected to pay for. When you lived abroad, perhaps a car or two came with the job, housing was provided free, school fees were paid, and trips home were covered.

New expenses challenge the lifestyle and budget of the average family. Expectations may have to be lowered and realistic limits set on the returnees' spending power. Just setting up home again can be an expensive business. Knowing where and how to obtain help is vital. There may be allowances from the government, grants to help you in business, and favorably rated loans. Again, the research can be done in advance, particularly if you have the help of someone at the home end.

A missionary who returned to the United Kingdom after nine years in Tanzania wrote:

Occasionally we have some fun. We were invited to come to the bank for a service interview to see if we qualified for a special 'lifestyle' account [promotional line of credit]. The conversation went like this:

"So, how much will you spend on lifestyle purchases this year?"

"Um, pass."

"How about holidays, flights, and travel?"

"Er, we'll visit friends."

"What about clothes?"

"Depends where we buy them." (Do charity shops count?)

"And home improvements?"

"Hard to say. Which home?"

At this stage we pointed out that maybe our lifestyle was not the one targeted by this sort of account, and perhaps it would be best to draw things to a close.

HOUSING

One of the biggest stresses upon return is finding somewhere not just to live but to *settle*. Because housing decision may be tied to a job search and getting children into schools, it can get complicated. Some people have houses to sell in the area where they previously worked, and, depending on the state of the housing market, they may find it takes quite some time to process that.

Arranging utilities like water, electricity, and garbage collection can take time too, and there is always a plethora of companies wanting to provide you with those services. When you are desperate just to receive these services, it can be difficult to make informed decisions. Again, this is where friends back home can help smooth the way. In the meantime, you may have to cope with the frustration of not having amenities others take for granted.

After several years in the bush, one couple said: "When we first arrived in our rented house, we had no telephone, no television, no radio, and no computer. Of course, it isn't easy to get a phone connected when you haven't got a phone apparatus, and in those few days spent on the edge of this new way of life, we realized that it is these technologies that provide the 'space' where people live today."

Many, particularly those who left at short notice, may have nowhere to stay except with a relative in what may be fairly close conditions. This can prove a strain on the relationships for all concerned. One family returning after a coup in an African republic remarked: "The hardest thing about coming back was having to be at home with my parents all the time, living together with our four girls."

For singles, finding a home may be more important than for families who have each other and for whom these relationships are the first and foremost place of security. One single lady, who retired after forty-two years overseas, said: "I was too busy to think about retirement, and I preferred not to. The biggest help was in the marvelous provision of my perfectly adapted flat. Knowing where I would be living was a great help in facing the whole subject of re-entry."

FAMILY NEEDS

Being in temporary accommodations also means children have to be in temporary schools. Children who find it difficult to make friends and settle into a different educational system may take longer to adjust. Returning to the United Kingdom after successive evacuations from Liberia and the Ivory Coast, one mother lamented: "Our children had to go to different schools as we were just out of the catchment area of our chosen one. Also, they had to start in the middle of the school year."

The family that returned from France to England said: "There was uncertainty as we looked for housing, tried to get the girls registered in the school of our choice, and moved and settled into our flat."

Exercising educational choice can be a real problem from a distance. Here again, a network of people who live locally, who know the system, and who can get you registered can be a great help. All of this is impossible, however, if you don't know where you will be settling. A parent who had children in local, national schools and at boarding schools overseas offered the following advice, with the benefit of hindsight: "Spend time with the whole family, together, planning for the return, both 'on-field' and back in the home country. We were unable to do this as the family was split between two countries and had less than three weeks to pack up and say goodbye and returned in two 'waves' due to courses which had to be finished."

Many people have commented on the difficulties their children faced on returning. Although the second section of this book is designed for TCKs, parents are permitted to read it too! But it is important that children are considered when making decisions and plans. The older they are, the more choices they need to be given in the matter. For some children, it is important that they finish their education in the place where they received most of their schooling. This may mean parents consider leaving them behind when they relocate. Certainly, this is an option for the family to consider together.

One boy had done all his schooling at an international school with a North American curriculum. The most important year was the last, when he had the chance to graduate, celebrate with all his friends, and enjoy the perks of the school. Just before this much-anticipated senior year, his parents decided to relocate back home to give him a year to settle before going to the university. They made this decision without consulting with their son or explaining their reasoning. For years he held it against them, feeling they had deprived him of that special year. It was only much later, as an adult, that he came to appreciate that they had made the decision for his benefit; but it would not have been *his* choice.

Much of what an adult expatriate feels in reviewing his or her own culture is what strikes children even more forcibly and increases their sense of frustration and alienation. A Scotsman married to a Canadian and returning from Europe commented: "We feel that people here are very monocultural. This is one of the biggest frustrations to fitting in. This has especially affected our girls, as they see this in their peers and feel so different and ultimately not really accepted."

Children also need a lot of help with their social adjustment. Language, especially knowing the latest slang, is particularly important, as are social activities—where it is safe to go socially, what skills are needed to participate, how much it costs to go out, what you are expected to pay for gifts, and to whom you are expected to give gifts. Children need help with practical skills as well as with cultural knowledge. The doctor with three girls returning from Thailand said: "The children were more confused by the U.K. than we were. They needed help with buses (they had only traveled by air or on a bicycle), shops, etc. We watched a lot of *East Enders* (a TV soap opera), which helped us to understand the culture and life that they needed to know about."

TCKs themselves provide advice on how to help them adjust to their new life at the end of Part II, but this parent whose children had been in small, national schools in Africa summed it up pretty well: "Children need a lot of time to adjust and discuss what is going on around them, including the use of language and avoiding much talk about where they have been and why. It is boring to others and can cause ostracism. In our case, team sports were good entries for our children. The local college was not a good social entry point. There is little social life surrounding it and students had their friends from school days and their part of the city."

SOCIAL SKILLS

Children may have problems fitting in, but so do adults, especially if they have subconsciously slipped into different ways of talking and behaving. This can lead to humorous and embarrassing situations. Perhaps a "how-not-to course" could help. Here are some suggestions:

- **How Not to Say It.** "I remember on a couple of occasions asking someone if they were pregnant and another if they were breastfeeding the new baby. They nearly dropped dead at such a *direct* question! Here things like that are only mentioned with close friends. I've learned to keep my mouth shut. In Brazil everyone speaks their mind, and questions like that are everyday conversation."

- **How Not to Do It.** "We returned to the same house we lived in before going out, so I knew the city quite well. On my first time walking in the city center, a man stopped to ask directions, and without thinking I took him by the hand to take him where he wanted to go. I think the expression on his face then was gob-smacked, and he backed away sharply. I think I may have been close to being arrested, yet in our host culture in Africa, nobody would have thought twice at holding a stranger's hand and leading them to their destination."

- **How Not to Look.** "I realized that when showing people things or places, I often pointed with my mouth or lips, as customary in our host culture, rather than using my forefinger. I don't know what folk thought, but I got some very strange looks until I caught on to what I was doing. I immediately stopped my Mick Jagger impressions!"

- **How Not to Win Friends.** "Staying with a friend, I managed in one weekend to put a gold-rimmed mug in the thing called a microwave, put petrol in her diesel car, and cut through the wire of her electric hedge-cutter. I can't believe she's still a good friend!"

- **How Not to Drive.** "After the African bush, driving in England was generally quite a breeze, but finding the way was exhausting. On one occasion I was following a car through Birmingham. All went well until we got into a lot of traffic, and my guide disappeared in Spaghetti Junction. He realized he had lost me and came back. For the next forty minutes, we went round and round the junction, frequently passing each other on opposite sides of the dual carriageway. Oh, for the African bush roads!"

- **How Not to Shop.** "My mother sent me to the local supermarket to buy some butter. Dazzled by the array of goods on the shelves, I noticed—*eggs*! We had not had eggs in Algeria for six months, so I bought two dozen. My triumphant return with these trophies was greeted by my mother with the words 'Oh no! I always buy free-range eggs from the milkman!'"

SPIRITUAL NEEDS

For some people, their time overseas was the result of a sense of vocation, and they may have a host of other questions and issues to deal with upon return.

- **Why didn't things work out?** "Why did we have to leave the place we felt we were meant to be?"

- **What does guidance mean?** "Is it right to make a pragmatic decision rather than getting specific guidance from God? Did we make the right decision at the right time? Why wasn't God making it clearer?"

- **Why wasn't I appreciated?** "Because I felt unwanted by Zambian staff, I almost 'sneaked away,' thinking that they would be glad if I left."

- **Why didn't anyone understand?** "I suffered burn-out after a hard struggle to get a new program of activity off the ground. The director of the international mission was fairly new to the job. His response to my needs was overbearing, and I was unable to shake him off."

- **Why should my family suffer?** "I felt loss, turmoil, confusion, and anger at what had been done to our family and at the mess we had been obliged to leave behind."

- **Why should I be different from my national friends?** "I felt a deep sense of being out of control and at the mercy of circumstances; and the questions of the moral rightness of leaving, when national colleagues could not, haunted me for a long time."

None of these questions has an easy answer, but they deserve honest consideration from those returning and those in churches and agencies on the receiving end. The worst possible response is to sweep them under the carpet and pretend they don't exist. For most people who responded to my questions (and many did so with amazing frankness that opened up some areas of considerable pain), what was most helpful was finding someone who would listen to them, accept them as they were without making judgments on how they were feeling, and give them time and space to work things through.

One woman's church gave her six months of paid leave to recover from a traumatic situation. A member of the house church of another lady asked to meet with her each week to talk and pray together. They became close friends and are still continuing the practice five years later. She said: "I valued very much being treated as a real person rather than as 'our worker who has come home.' I needed that close contact, as other friends had moved on."

In all these areas, the more you can anticipate the changes, the better you will cope with them. What follows is a selection of advice from those who have experienced re-entry themselves.

- Plan as much as you can for the differences and be aware that people back home, in the main, won't understand or be interested in what you have been doing.

- Make up your mind to turn the page and enjoy your new stage of life. While maintaining relationships with those you love and have left behind, decide not to cling to the past.

- Do not be in a hurry to fill your life with new activities. Wait until you know what you want to do.

- Try to find someone who can identify with your past ministry and to whom you can speak without having to explain things all the time or feel guilty for talking about your overseas experiences.

- Try to settle where you know people. There are no shortcuts to feeling comfortable.

- Be patient with yourself and don't make major decisions right away.

- Take time to prepare. It is tough, but you will make it.

- Allow yourself time to settle. Don't overcommit.

- It's an opportunity to try something new, but the transition is difficult.

- Give yourself time. Don't expect too much too soon.

> I sometimes catch myself looking up at the moon, remembering the changes of fortune in our long voyage, thinking of the thousands of people who had worked to bring the three of us home. (*Apollo 13*, the film)

— 5 —

DEBRIEFING

I was shocked, but not altogether surprised, to read that of those who responded to my questionnaire, 80 percent received no preparation or help before their return. Significantly, those who had been given an opportunity to debrief listed it high on their advice-to-follow list. Many regretted not having an opportunity to unpack emotionally with someone who understood. They may not have used or understood the word *debrief*, but that was what they were talking about. However, the organizations responsible for their assignments would often say that they did provide preparation and debriefing. So who is telling the truth?

The fact is that what the organization may see as preparation and debriefing from its perspective—a time to inform returnees on what they did well and what they could do better—does not always match up to the individual's needs and expectations. Sometimes this is because those in management have no experience of overseas assignments themselves and are, therefore, unaware of the issues surrounding re-entry. Often, those in the head office do not see the personal needs of returning staff as their responsibility, particularly if there is no continuing role for them within the organization.

Many organizations do not have anyone who is trained in debriefing procedures, someone who understands the need for a structured session and the areas that should be covered. Critically, some are not aware of the need, and others are just not willing to pay for sending returning staff to an outside consultant who can be objective and impartial and, therefore, trusted by the returnee.

For much of this chapter, I have drawn on the expertise of Dr. Debbie Lovell-Hawker, at the time a clinical psychologist working out of Warnford Hospital, Oxford, England.[1]

DEFINITION OF DEBRIEFING

Debriefing is an opportunity for returnees to tell their stories, to express their feelings about assignments and their performances, to evaluate their experiences, and to address grievances. It is a chance for them to analyze the stages of re-entry through which they are passing and the associated problems. There are three types of debriefing:

- **Operational Debriefing.** This relates to the task and involves asking for information about the work performed and what was achieved. This can be done

by someone in the same company who is familiar
with the objectives of the assignment.

- **Personal Debriefing.** This addresses such questions
as: How was the experience for the individual?
What was the best and worst thing about the
assignment? How is the readjustment process
going? The aim is to help returnees integrate their
experiences into their lives as a whole, perceive
the experiences meaningfully, and bring a sense of
closure. It is best carried out by someone outside
the organization.

Very often when people come home, their major
problem is with the organization or someone
who works for it. Expressing concerns to senior
management or the in-house personnel department
is difficult and threatening, especially if the returnee
hopes to continue working for the same company.
Returnees do not want to jeopardize their careers by
expressing concerns, and yet, in order to move on,
the returnees need to deal with their feelings.

- **Critical-Incident Debriefing.** This is a highly
structured form of personal debriefing, which can
take place after a traumatic experience such as a
natural disaster, war, violent incident, or traffic
accident. There are many reactions to severe stress,
and it helps to know what these are. Professional
help at an early stage helps to resolve issues more
satisfactorily and prevent long-term effects.

THE USE OF DEBRIEFING

For various reasons, an overseas assignment may have been stressful. Stress comes from cross-cultural living, unfamiliar customs, different value systems, as well as tensions in management and operational styles. Even if the stress is only slightly more than that experienced in a mono-cultural situation, the experience is likely to have made a profound impact on the individual's life and challenged many previously held beliefs and assumptions.

For this reason, it is important to give returnees the opportunity to express their reactions to what they have experienced and to begin assimilating the experience. In general, those who have been properly debriefed have valued the experience, even if they would not, at first, have elected to be debriefed.

Debriefing has many positive aspects. First, it is reassuring. It helps individuals know that it is normal to experience minor difficulties while readjusting. It reduces their worry at what they are experiencing. Debriefing can reduce the sense of isolation expatriates often feel on returning to their countries of origin. They realize they are not alone in experiencing these feelings. There is a normal curve of emotions accompanying the experience.

Second, debriefing is preventative. Because it allows uninhibited, nonjudgmental expression of feelings, it may help prevent depression or anxiety disorders from developing. It helps deal with feelings of failure or guilt. Any stress-related symptoms and adjustment difficulties can be noticed and addressed. An experienced debriefer will know when to recommend professional help and where to seek that help.

Third, debriefing affirms a person's worth. Many who were not offered any sort of debriefing spoke of feeling worthless, undervalued, and unsupported. Debriefing shows that they are valued, cared for, and their contribution means something. As issues are resolved and closure is achieved, people can move on with their lives.

Next, debriefing helps the company. Although a debriefing is primarily for the individual, companies can learn and change on the basis of what they hear. Although what is said will be confidential, and although the primary goal of debriefing is to help the individual rather than benefit the organization, it is possible that the organization will receive some feedback from the participant. Moreover, an organization that cares enough for its people to provide a debriefing process will have a better profile and attract more supporters.

Last, debriefing is recommended by the People-in-Aid Code of Good Practice. People in Aid is a worldwide affiliation of agencies involved in humanitarian activities.[2] Organizations that fail to offer debriefing may in the future be refused funding or visas and volunteers. Staff may select those organizations that do adhere to the Code of Good Practice.

HOW TO DEBRIEF

Once an organization has accepted the validity and value of debriefing, several questions arise in deciding the most effective way to undertake the exercise. Debriefing does not require a mental health professional, but it does require the debriefer to have a sound knowledge of the issues involved and the best way of making this a positive encounter. It is important that at the end of the meeting there is a sense of closure and of moving on to the next stage of life.

The first area to be considered is the timing of a debriefing session. When people have just returned from overseas, they first need time to adjust to their home country. In this case, debriefing is best done in the first few weeks after the return. If this is not possible, debriefing at another point is still useful. A follow-up contact three weeks later may also be beneficial. Critical-incident debriefing should take place twenty-four to seventy-two hours after the event. The debriefing process usually requires a few hours. It is important that this process is not rushed and that adequate time is set aside to validate the returnee's experiences and feelings.

Second, the organization should make sure that the debriefer is competent. The debriefer should be someone who has knowledge of the culture the participant was based in, experience in debriefing, and, preferably, some overseas experience. Gender may be an issue in some cases and cultures. It is very important that a debriefer be a good listener and not be judgmental. This is not the time to investigate procedures to see how things were done. Empathy is the quality required. At this stage, it is not essential that debriefers be medically qualified, although they should have enough awareness about the significance of symptoms to know when to bring in a professional.

Third, there is the question of whether this should be an individual or group debriefing. When an event has affected a group of people (for instance, evacuation), it can be most helpful to debrief as a group. In that case, it is ideal if everybody in the group attends. Experiences and feelings may be interrelated. Otherwise, people seem to prefer to be debriefed individually or with their partners. When a group is debriefed together, a more complete picture emerges of what actually took place. Because of personalities, vantage points, and degrees of involvement, different people see different aspects of an event. Having the wider input from the group can reinforce (or challenge) the perceptions of an individual.

Last, careful consideration should be given to the location for a debriefing. It should take place in a comfortable room where there will be no interruptions. The returnees need to feel secure and safe while working through their issues. In the case of a critical-incident debriefing, the debriefing helps to hold it near the site, although this may not be practical.

When organizations offer debriefing, people should be free to either take advantage of or opt out of it. If debriefing is not offered and returnees ask for it, they may be perceived as having a problem. However, if debriefing is the norm, then there is no stigma attached.

THE POWER OF DEBRIEFING

I found that people appreciated debriefing, even if they weren't eager when it was first offered to them. Some, in fact, wanted to come back for more. They found that knowledge, especially self-knowledge, is empowering. It helps to know:

- **This season will end!** Changes are to be expected, and further changes are to come. Readjustment periods often include tiredness, crying in the middle of the day, loss of appetite, depression, loneliness, and feelings of isolation.

- **People who do not relieve their stress are often accident prone.** Keeping a diary can be good for overall health. Journaling can lead to the increase of white blood cells, thus improving the immune system. For others, talking about experiences is even better than journaling. Relieving emotions through tears can have a cleansing effect. It has been chemically demonstrated that tears of sadness contain toxins that the body has been storing.

- **People need to give themselves permission to embrace all their emotions.** They need to know where to go for help, which books to read and websites to visit, and they need to know how to handle the stories no one wants to hear.

CHILDREN AND DEBRIEFING

Many children returning from an overseas posting are *very angry*. They are angry at their parents for removing them, angry at the political situation that caused it, angry at the company that recalled their parents, angry at the friends they left behind, angry at people trying to befriend them in a place they don't want to be, and angry at God for not doing things differently.

It is just as important for children to articulate how they feel and have someone listen as it is for adults. And because parents are in the middle of transition themselves, they may have neither the time nor the energy to cope with their children's emotions. So it is even more necessary to provide a qualified person outside of the family to sit down and spend time with the children.

Like their parents, children need to know they are valued and listened to. They need to know that someone cares about how they feel and what they have been through. They need to find someone safe to whom they can voice their fears and frustrations. They need avenues through which they can express their emotions and anxieties.

Even small children have fears they may not be prepared to voice to their parents. One little boy on seeing the "sold" sign go up outside his house said: "Will we have to live in a tent forever?" In a debriefing session, small children can be helped to express their anxieties and emotions through creative play, games, puppets, artwork, and telling stories.

Children may need more hugs and comfort than usual. At the same time, they may feel abandoned by their parents who are busy setting up a home and restoring their lifestyle. Being able to express such feelings without fear of hurting their parents is an enormous relief. Polly Chan, in *Doing Member Care Well*, said: "Children can feel the pain and they do not need to wait until they grow up to reflect on the experience and do something about the wounds."[3]

Like adults, children can be educated to know that what they are going through is normal and valid. Debriefing provides children the opportunity to ask for information they need and to be given resources to find that information. Children can also be helped to look on the positive side of the situation and anticipate what will be good in the future, while affirming the past.

HOW TO FOLLOW UP

In certain circumstances, it may be appropriate for the organization to have a follow-up session, but, generally, the onus is on the individual to take it from there. It helps if the debriefer produces some sort of summary of the session, including points to work on. Even if there are to be no further sessions, the individual can make a timetable to check up on the progress made and follow through on suggestions. Generally, debriefing opens up new avenues of living and establishes confidence for making a fresh, clean start.

With children who have been in a difficult or traumatic situation, it is important to establish regular routines as soon as possible. Activities that are familiar provide comfort and reassurance. These include the resumption of bedtime routines, mealtimes, returning to school, taking part in group activities, sports, and clubs. Children will need the security and comfort of their parents' attention, but they also require the freedom to continue to express their feelings and thoughts about what has happened.

Parents may need a lot of patience, since children's behavior may become very difficult and demanding. Small children may be clingy. Parents need to be aware of the normal stages of childhood development so that they can separate the abnormal behaviors from the normal ones.

Responses to traumatic situations may include regressive behavior, rebelliousness, irritability, sleep disturbances, recurring dreams, bladder problems, speech difficulties, loss of appetite, and withdrawal from society. Recognizing these is the first step to helping children find a place where they can talk about their fears, recount their dreams, and recall their memories. As with adults, it is important to help children normalize their feelings and teach them coping strategies.

Richard W. Bagge, in a paper entitled "Traumatic Stress and Families," said: "Part of the task of an individual is to find a means of expression by which they can transform their pain, internal conflicts, and feelings into words and other forms of expression. Art, drawing, painting, journaling, drama, and story telling are helpful as soon as the individual is capable of meaningful interaction with the medium."[4]

Responsibilities at home and school may need to be modified for a period of time. Structure is helpful, but it needs to be flexible. It is important to have open channels of communication where nothing is taboo; however, it is important to respect a child's right to privacy, especially in the case of adolescents.

One parent with three teenage children advised:

> Parents need to spend lots of time with kids re-acculturating by visiting shops, schools, and recreational activities. Most important, though, if they are to make friends quickly, is to watch lots of soap opera (no matter how gross you find it) and watch or listen to chart music. You need to watch *with* them because the standards portrayed for life and behavior will probably be very different from those they are used to in a mission or expatriate context. They need to be able to discuss the issues portrayed in a nonjudgmental way with their parents.

JUDGING THE BENEFITS

It is not easy to conduct research that randomly assigns people to either be debriefed or not, and then follow up both groups. Of the studies done so far, the findings have varied, but they had major methodological flaws. Overseas development workers who have been debriefed upon their return home have found it beneficial. It is particularly helpful when *all* employees and members are debriefed, not just those perceived as having had problems. A middle-aged man who did not initially see the need for a debriefing reported afterward: "I had thought beforehand it was going to be a waste of time, but I found that actually it was very helpful to be able to talk about everything, however small, that had happened."

Many experienced a positive change afterward. They spoke of "a sense of relief," "permission to feel the way I was feeling," and "deciding to seek counseling." The opportunity to debrief provides a place where the experience can be normalized and closure effected on the time overseas. This then puts the returnees in the place where they are ready to move on. Good endings make for good beginnings.

At every turn in the road a new illumining is needed to find the way and a new kindling is needed to follow the way. (John Dunne)

Part II

THIRD CULTURE KIDS: CATCHING THE WAVES

INTRODUCTION

"I feel like I'm a nomad. I have no real home. I'm trying to find out where I fit in. Sometimes I feel like I'm an alien!"

"Home is a very relative word for me. Right now my parents live in Hungary, so in a sense that is home. I've lived most of my life in the U.K., so in another sense that is home. I'm an American, and so in yet another sense, America is home."

"When we came home, I felt grief—utter grief! Sadness! Depression! Nothing nice, really."

Have you ever felt like that? When did you come back to your parents' home country? Does it feel like home to you? If you could be anywhere in the world, where would that be?

If you can identify with those statements, then welcome to the Society of Third Culture Kids! You're not a strange being, an alien species. There are thousands like you out there, all feeling the same, most wishing they knew someone who understood what it's like.

One day I was at an international conference, walking behind a TCK from Morocco. She had been to a summer camp made up almost exclusively of kids who had been brought up overseas. I couldn't help overhearing her tell a TCK friend: "The camp was wonderful. You didn't have to *explain yourself* to anyone!"

The next few chapters are to help you see through the mist and discover your unique identity, appreciate the specialness of being a TCK, and also work through some of the challenges that it represents. You may have been back for some years now, but never fully understood who you are or where you fit in. Or, you may have only recently returned and are feeling as if you've been caught up in a whirlwind with things spiralling out of control. Some of you may have been quite young when you arrived, but the memories and experiences are still vivid in your mind and heart. Some have only returned for tertiary education and are conscious of the gap between you and your monocultural peers—culturally, emotionally, and developmentally.

These chapters will not only help you unpack the experience of being a TCK but will also give you practical tips on surviving the experience—and not just survive but *thrive* in your cross-cultural identity.

Rather than using the space metaphor, I've chosen the surfing analogy here. A surfer waits to catch the best waves and then rides them to the shore. A surfer can take quite a buffeting on the way, but it's an exhilarating experience. It can be quite dangerous too. You have to keep from being hurt by your own surfboard or the pounding surf. But nothing beats the thrill of getting it right. And surfing is best done in the company of other surfers who care about how you're doing and will exchange tips on how to get the most out of the experience.

So, what do you need to be a surfer? Read on!

Windsurfing gets into your blood and in your soul. At first it's just traipsing round with a small rig. Soon it starts being a little more in depth and you find yourself wanting to experience all the excitement it has to offer. Then before you know you're hooked and it's crazy. Maybe you start wearing strange clothing, talking in a dialect only known by people with similar clothing. It has the power to take over your life and control your every mood and emotion. (*The Ultimate Guide to Windsurfing*)[1]

— 6 —

WHO AM I?

When I was growing up, adults always asked me what I was going to be, but there came a time when what I was going to be wasn't as important as who I was. Everyone questions who they are and TCKs are no exception.

Who is a TCK? I am a combination of two cultures. I am neither, and I am both. I am the brat who throws a temper tantrum and refuses to dress native for the American church. I am the one who desperately worries about fitting in, but I am the one who wears my native wrap around the college dorm and doesn't care what anyone thinks.

I am the one who traveled halfway around the world before I was four, and I am the one who has no home. I am the one who promises to write but never does because it's too difficult to deal with the reality of separation. I am the one who speaks two languages but can't spell either.

I am the one who wears a thousand masks, one for each day and time. I am the one who learned to be all I'm expected to be, but is still not sure of who I really am. (Anonymous, a TCK)

DEFINITION OF THIRD CULTURE KID

So, what do we mean by Third Culture Kid? Third Culture Kid is a term coined in the 1950s by two social scientists, John and Ruth Hill Useem,[2] when they went to India to study North Americans who lived and worked there in a variety of jobs. According to the Useems, the first culture is the home culture from which the parents come. The second is the host culture in which they live. The third culture is the shared lifestyle of the expatriate community. The Useems described children who had in common the experience of growing up overseas as Third Culture Kids. If you want to understand the phenomenon in depth, then I suggest you read *Third Culture Kids* by David Pollock and Ruth Van Reken, or a shorter version in my book, *Families on the Move*.[3] I will briefly define this term:

A Third Culture Kid is an individual who, having
spent a significant part of the developmental years in
a culture other than the parents' culture, develops a
sense of relationship to all of the cultures while not
having full ownership of any. Elements from each
culture are incorporated into the life experience, but
the sense of belonging is in relationship to others of
similar experience.

It is generally understood that the phrase *significant part of
the developmental years* means two years or more in a culture
that is different from that of either parent. Of course, two years
spent between the ages of six months and two and a half years
will be less significant than two years spent between ages eight
and ten or twelve and fourteen. The effect on the child is also
determined by the degree to which the family has immersed itself
in the host culture.

By the phrase *develops a sense of relationship to all of the
cultures*, I mean that children absorb bits of each culture into their
personalities, affecting likes and dislikes, behavior and values. It
encompasses the things that are important in determining choices
and priorities.

For instance, if you were brought up in India, you will probably appreciate spicy food and bright colors. If you were raised
in Japan, you probably prefer your plain, rare food and conserva-
tive clothes and behavior. If you grew up in South America, you
may be quite a radical, identifying with the poor and the under-
privileged, and have a strong sense of social justice. Coming from
Africa, you may have a more carefree, laid-back attitude toward
life, resisting routines and time-keeping.

However, there are other parts of your character that don't belong to this type of category. There are other attitudes you have learned from your parents, your school (which may be another culture altogether), and from your other expatriate friends. You are a mixture of all these things, but you probably don't feel that you belong to any one of them. Your sense of belonging is more in relation to other individuals who have had similar experiences.

This means that the Third Culture is not a mixture of the two or more cultures among which you have grown up, but is the grouping of all those who share your experience, that is, all those who have grown up outside of their passport culture. It means you have far more in common with other TCKs, no matter where in the world they have grown up, than you do with your monocultural peers back home. Ruth Goring Stewart, in her poem "I am Green,"[4] likens the experience to having a pair of yellow glasses that represents your home culture, and having a pair of blue ones that represents your host culture; the resulting combination lens through which you see the world is green.

This is why no one really understands a TCK like another TCK. You will probably have a troubling sense of frustration with your home culture, resulting from the failure of people to see things any other way than the way they've always seen them and the failure of society to appreciate other valid ways of doing and looking at things.

And it doesn't matter in what capacity your family has been overseas. Children of those in the military, the diplomatic corps, charitable agencies, or relief work all go through the same process—unless they have been holed up on an expatriate compound with no contact with local culture, and that's difficult to do these days.

BENEFITS OF THE TCK EXPERIENCE

While you may have struggles when you return, there are huge benefits to growing up overseas. You've seen the world other people only read about. You've been there, smelled it, tasted it, and savored it. You've probably learned another language, not through school work but through living in the culture. You have the native accent because you learned it as a child.

One TCK who spent his early years in Japan said: "I know I have definitely gained from the experience in ways such as:

- Having a stronger stomach
- Cultural awareness that the West is not the only or right or best way
- Less culture shock now when I visit poorer countries
- Greater independence in life as a result of being in boarding school

You have probably become good at reaching out to people and have learned to make friends easily. You may have noticed that all around you people are on the move, not just your family. Consequently, there are always friends leaving and new kids arriving, as people come and go on vacation and new assignments. New relationships are always on the horizon. The downside to this is that you're also good at saying goodbye because that's a constant feature of your life. One defining statement about TCKs is: You'd rather never say hello than have to say goodbye.

Does that strike a chord within you? But remember, learning how to make good partings is a valuable life skill, because change is a constant part of life. As the world becomes a smaller place and people continually have to move for employment, the ability to close one situation and start well again in another is a marketable skill.

Cross-cultural skills are a valuable asset in the job market as globalization takes over the marketplace. People who can cross boundaries with ease, who appreciate cultural differences and respond appropriately, already have an advantage. Rather than apologize for your differences, capitalize on them. Ask yourself, "What does this give me that other people don't have?"

The other big plus is the enormous bank of friends that you have accumulated all over the world. Like you, they have moved around a lot and may be located on the other side of the world right now. But with e-mail and the Internet, the other side of the world is not so very far. Keeping in touch has never been easier. And if you want to go traveling, you'll never be without a place to stay.

CHALLENGES OF THE TCK EXPERIENCE

I am not saying that it's all easy for you. Saying goodbye too often can leave your heart raw and make you feel uneasy about entering into any relationship that calls for deep commitment. It's scary to do so in case this person leaves you like everyone else in your life has done. This is a hard thing to come to terms with when you need to make choices about life partners and settling down.

Career choice comes up against the same barrier. Up to now, you may have been used to making only short-term decisions. You could never see further down the road than the next two years, when your family might have to move again. Now you're faced with the decision of which subject to study at the university that will enable you to pursue the career of your choice. How do you know what you want to be doing in ten years, never mind twenty-five? Some of these options may not have existed when you were overseas. Perhaps you were never made aware of all the possibilities open to you.

You may be fluent in both your mother tongue and your acquired tongue, but in which have you been educated? If you never had to write essays in your mother tongue, then you could find yourself in academic trouble when you return home because your spoken ability may be much better than your writing ability. You may play catch-up for a while until you have a good grasp of the written language. One TCK who grew up in Africa was discouraged by her grades when she returned to England. She said: "I lived in Africa, but I was educated in German till I was fifteen. When I went to an English school, I knew the answers to all the teacher's questions—I just couldn't express them in English."

The poem at the beginning of this chapter echoes the feeling of many TCKs that they belong everywhere, but don't feel at home anywhere. "There's no place like home," says an old song, but home for TCKs is where the heart is. In other words, home is where the people you love are, rather than any particular place. So, relationships are very important, and it will probably always be important to you to know where your parents are.

At a seminar in London in 1999, Dave Pollock said: "Your heart tells you where home is. Your passport tells you where you legally belong. Home is where you can leave, come back to, and leave again."

DISCOVERING YOURSELF

I'm assuming many of the things you've read in this chapter strike a chord, and you're saying, "Yes, that's me!" If so, then you probably want to move from the general to the specific. So far, we've looked at what you share in common with all TCKs, but what about your particular identity? What has gone into making you *you*? How can you put the pieces together in a way that makes sense to you and helps you decide how to fit into the new situation in which you find yourself?

Maybe it's best to start with a bit of biography to find out where you've come from and how you got to this place. Try answering the following questions:

- Where were my parents born?
  Where have my parents lived before and since I was born?

- Where was I born?
  How long did I live there?

- Where was my first school?
  What was it like?

- When did I first learn a second language?
  What was it?
  How often did I use it and for how long?
  What language do I think and dream in?

- Where have I spent the longest single period of my life?

- What did I like best about the place I've come from? What am I most looking forward to in the new place? Of those I've left behind, whom will I miss most? Why?

- Where do I feel most comfortable—on my own or with lots of people? How do I enjoy spending my leisure time? Is that possible now that I'm back?

- What skills and abilities have I developed in my time overseas? How do I cope with change?

- What was the last move like for me? Complete the sentence: Change is . . .

The answers to those questions should give you a good idea of the sort of person you are and how you're going to cope with what lies ahead. For instance, if you've made lots of moves and they've all been good experiences, it's likely you'll manage this one well also. If, on the other hand, you've had some gruesome times because of moving, you'll probably expect the worst with this one and be anxious at the prospect.

It's important to know your likes and dislikes, because although these may be the product of where you have lived, in the end, they are just preferences, not rights and wrongs. You don't have to apologize for them or give them up. They are part of your identity. However, you do have to realize that other people's likes and dislikes are equally valid and not judge them.

PUTTING YOUR LIFE BACK TOGETHER

In this poem called *Belonging*, a TCK wrote of her
experience:

Where is my home?
Where on earth do I belong?
In days gone by
Of childhood innocence and wonder?
Surrounded by cushioning pillows
Of life in a far away land?
Of life back "at home"?
Children played and laughter floated on the air.
I was free, not packaged into a box
Bolted back, into reality
Not to me it wasn't.
Unfamiliar faces professing to know me
Like my own mother.
Trapped and frightened was I.
There was no escape.
Reality hit.
A brick wall of pain.
Sadness at happy memories.
No. I couldn't go back?
WHY NOT? I screamed
Inside.
"I'm your best friend," "No, I am!"
New found *friends* vying for me,
The new girl's attention.

No! My best friends never were to be seen again.

Again I cried out WHY?

I WAS A MELTING POT OF MISERY.

Years of struggle with self identity,

An exhausting trek, an attempt to belong and to conform.

But then the real realization hit.

Something, somewhere said and smiled down on me,

"Accept, move on and be happy being YOU,

The wonderful, special, unique child you are!"

So I did.

I was and am always will be a WORLD CHILD.

Why not?

There are no boundaries to fence me in,

No walls.

My life is no longer that

Of sorrow with occasional joy.

I learned to be happy,

To be free in me.

(Miriam Dyer)[5]

For many TCKs, coming home feels like trying to put a square peg into a round hole—it doesn't fit and it feels like it never will. And there's a degree of truth in that. You never grow out of being a TCK—it's a lifetime experience. It's what has gone into making the person who is you, and there's no use denying it. However, in order to make a life for yourself, you do have to find ways of integrating this experience into the life that lies before you.

There are two sides to this. One is daring to be different, and the other is learning how to belong. There's nothing wrong in being different. You don't have to submit to peer pressure to be just like all the rest. However, you are probably going to have to make some important decisions. What values are you willing to lay aside in order to fit into this society of which you are now a part? Our values are the priorities that govern the decisions we make, the friends we choose, and our preferences. Which things are really essential to your being, things you're not going to give up at any cost? At the very least, you might have to give up your desire to eat curry every night of the week, recognizing that when you go out in a crowd, you often have to compromise with other people's choices.

Those sorts of decisions can be trivial, but they can also be painful. I know of a family that has been back from Thailand for years, and their preference is still Thai food when they can get the proper ingredients. Some TCKs grow up in places where it is important to always have people around you. The formality in most homes in the Western world is hard to accept if you've been used to a society where the door is always open and you can drop in at any time. Living in an apartment at a university can be a lonely experience when you have been used to living in community.

Learning to belong takes time and patience. For those returning for higher education, I think it's a good idea to take a year off when you return. Many non TCK students these days take a year off before embarking on a course of study and spend it traveling overseas. The reverse is good for TCKs. If you spend a year back in your home country earning some money or doing volunteer work, you can learn the way things work, watch how it's done, and make your mistakes in a place where no one knows you. If you go straight to college and make cultural *faux pas* there, your classmates may laughingly remind you of these for the next three years.

Learning takes good observation skills, watching how others do it and finding someone to steer you through the minefield. It's really best if you can set this up before you come home. Find a friend of the family, roughly the same age as you, who is prepared to spend time with you and show you around. This person can explain what to do and why.

MAKING CHOICES

I've already said how hard it is for TCKs to make choices. Many feel that over the years the ability to choose has been taken from them. They had no choice but to follow wherever their parents took them. Sometimes decisions were made for their benefit but never fully explained to them. One boy's family came home for the sake of his education, believing that the local schooling would not qualify him for further education in his home country. However, this was not the case. The diploma he would have gained would have been recognized by the home country's universities. Alternatively, he could have gone to boarding school in the host country, but his parents never offered that option. *They* thought they were doing the right thing. As it turned out, he hated the new situation. And if he had been offered the opportunity to board locally, he would have grabbed it with both hands, and done anything to stay where he was.

You might return from overseas because you didn't have access to information that would enable you to make a choice that was meaningful. For instance, if your school only teaches a limited range of subjects, you may never have had the opportunity to try out some subject that you could go on to study and enjoy. What was the career information like at your school? Did it offer you a full range of options and advice on what was available? And did it tell what qualifications you would need to pursue that career?

Have you chosen your school or college from overseas without ever having visited it? Do you know what sort of area it's in? Is it out in the countryside, miles from anywhere? Is it in the middle of a city? Or, is it on a campus outside of the city, self-contained and separate from the real world? What if you get there and find you don't like it at all? You can get some pretty good virtual tours on the Web today, but nothing beats an on-site visit. If there's any way that you can make such a visit before you decide, take it. It may mean coming back the summer before you finish school or deferring your selection until you return.

Choice without information is no choice at all. You have to know what is open to you and what is possible for you. This may involve looking at the financial implications of your choice. Where is the money coming from to fund it? What funding are you eligible for? How do you apply for scholarships? Some of these questions need to be looked at long before you return. Keeping academic records is very important when you are making applications.

Most of the TCKs I know are very positive about their overseas experiences—they wouldn't have missed them for the world. But they are realistic about the pain and cost involved and the difficulty of re-entry, which, for many, is the hardest part. In the next chapter we will look at how to handle the pain and emotions of moving back. But you move back in order to move on.

> Don't underestimate how much strength, fitness and agility are needed to survive the pounding of big waves. The trick is never to underestimate nature but always be realistic about your own limitations. Before you tackle nature you have to tackle the battle in your own mind. To improve you have to push yourself beyond your comfort zone. It is a question of whether you want to push yourself beyond that warm and cozy place in the search for success. (*The Ultimate Guide to Windsurfing*, page 36)

— 7 —

THE EMOTIONAL ROLLER COASTER

"How many times can you have a piece of your heart torn out without finally dying?" (anonymous TCK).

We all have our own ways of responding to change, trauma, and transition. Universally, the emotion that dominates the return home of a TCK is *grief*. Moving back is just one more loss added to all those that have gone before—the loss of friends who have moved on, the loss of house and school, and the loss of cultural signposts. But this loss is permanent; there may never be a chance to return. This is a form of death, and death requires mourning, saying goodbye, acknowledging the pain and hurt, facing the future without what you have lost, and taking the time to process all the emotion.

The problem is that when you return to your country of passport, there is so much to do that you can't take the time you need to grieve and process what you're going through. Sometimes, years later an event, a smell, or a chance conversation will trigger a response that you don't understand. Then the pain of the past rears its head and you don't know how to handle it. Or else, the grief turns to anger, bitterness, and resentment that cloak the real pain. Anger is a symptom that often covers other feelings such as hurt, bitterness, grief, and fear.

The whole family is busy upon return. Parents are finding jobs and somewhere to live, buying furniture and groceries, setting up a home, dealing with bureaucracies, filling out forms to get services, and a hundred other things. They are suffering grief and bereavement themselves and might not have the time or energy to cope with the angst you are going through. So children learn to bottle up their emotions, batten down the hatches, and get on with life.

Apart from the danger of postponing grief recovery until the future, there is also the real possibility of serious depression setting in. Individuals suffering from loneliness, isolation, and alienation are prime candidates for shutting themselves away and being caught in a depressive spiral, which has serious consequences for their long-term health and well-being. The aim of this chapter is to help you unpack those emotions safely and recognize the normality of your experience and the symptoms that are danger signs.

REVISITING THE PAST

You can only move on in life when you face up to the person you are and where you have come from. Hopefully, learning about the TCK profile is a good place to start. But you then need to look closer at what has gone on in your life and how you feel about the place where you are now. As I have already said, many TCKs are faced with multiple separations and losses in their lives. Some have been sent away to school and never really recovered from that separation. One TCK, who had been sent home to boarding school when she was six, remarked:

> I made Mum's life a misery when they came back when I was fourteen. I felt like I had to catch up on eight years of missed time—all those years that I had been at boarding school. Between the ages of fourteen and seventeen, it was as though I regressed back being six and then I had to catch back up with myself. Thankfully, I managed to do this by seventeen. Maybe there is an element in this of being a teenager anyway, but I did have conscious thought about wanting to make up for lost time.

As a part of revisiting your past, I encourage you to reflect on the following questions:

- How many moves have you made?
- How old were you when they happened?

- Why did you have to move?

- How were those moves for you?

- How do you feel about the separations?

- Did you handle them well?

- How do you feel about this last move? Is there an element of resentment?

Consider drawing a chart with a column for each year of your life; use a different color each time you made a move, whether it was for an extended vacation or a new assignment. You might be surprised at the multicolored landscape that emerges.

Not only is separation an issue, but many TCKs feel like victims. Decisions were made over which they had no control and no say, but that affected them profoundly. For instance, the changes in education and lifestyle and the timing of the moves all affected their development.

If you feel like a victim, then you are a prime candidate for feeling bitter. Here you are at a stage in your life when *you* should be making significant choices about friends, activities, and education. However, previous choices made by your parents on your behalf mean that many of these decisions are out of your control.

A North American TCK who had grown up in South Korea said: "I'm sick of making friends and always saying goodbye. You made me do this in the country I grew up in, then you dragged me back to the States to a school that I hate; at least now I have friends, and now I'm going to have to leave them. Even if I make friends in the new country we're going to (which you told me I would in the States and I didn't), I will have to say goodbye to them again."

Many people have strong feelings about the changes brought about by re-entry and protest is natural. In time these strong emotions will pass or become less painful.

Inevitably, attachment also becomes an issue. The more moves you make, the harder it is to get attached. Think of how many broken attachments there have been in your life. Broken attachments lead to lack of trust. The pattern goes like this:

- You have a need; you express that need.
- The need does not get fully met—the person is too busy or goes away.
- You learn not to trust anyone.
- You become good at meeting your own needs.
- You only form superficial relationships.

John Ruskin, the British art critic and author, said: "Men are more evanescent than pictures, yet one sorrows for lost friends and pictures are my friends. I have none others. I am never long enough with men to attach myself to them; and whatever feelings of attachment I have are to material things."[1]

Here are more questions to help you reflect on your past so you can better understand your present:

- How many close relationships have you had?
- How long did they last?

- Do you have a lack of trust in others?

- To whom have you turned to meet your needs?

- Do you hold people at arm's length?

- How do you break off a friendship? Do you get angry?

- Are you afraid of commitment?

- Do you need to be in control and fear being manipulated?

- How do you feel about physical expressions of affection?

Learning about your emotional framework helps you understand why you react as you do and helps you move to the point where you can become committed and make genuine attachments. One TCK whose parents moved regularly with the military remarked: "Because of the way I grew up, I tend to not go very deep into relationships . . . because it hurts too much if you have to leave them. And you know you will have to leave them eventually."

Similarly, there can be a real loss of self-esteem if you feel you've been moved around a lot, and no one really cared what you thought or how you felt. This goes along with feeling rootless, invisible, abandoned, and of no account. A feeling of "not having mattered" can lead you to try to become "somebody" by doing dangerous or unwise things, trying to impress your peers by being more reckless than they are. Alternatively, you may bury yourself in a life of service, being the doormat you perceive yourself to be.

There's nothing wrong with a life of service, provided it is done from the right motives.

To help you sort out these feelings, consider the questions below:

- Have I ever felt abandoned or discounted as an individual?
- Have I been involved in family discussions on the future?
- Is there anything I am good at?
- Do I always compare myself unfavorably with others?
- How do I seek to impress people?
- Who made me feel good as a child and why?

PROCESSING EMOTIONS

There are certain natural reactions in the cycle of grief. The grief itself is a natural reaction to the return from overseas. Sadness, loss, and isolation are the typical feelings expressed by TCKs. Anger is a natural stage of grief, anger at this tearing away, at the people perceived as causing this loss, and at life itself. If you get stuck in the anger phase, then you can't move on and the anger becomes bitterness, resentment, and may lead to clinical depression. The anger and grief have to be processed to enable a new beginning.

I want to suggest four Ps to process emotions: (1) permission to feel pain, (2) permission to express feelings, (3) pathways to saying goodbye, and (4) people to share experiences.

Permission to Feel Pain

United States congresswoman Maxine Waters said: "I have a right to my anger, and I don't want anybody telling me I shouldn't be, that it's not nice to be, and that something's wrong with me because I get angry."[2]

Saying goodbye is painful, but pain is often good for us. We feel pain when we touch something hot, and that warns us to be careful. If we have pains in the chest, we'd better see the doctor. Physical pain has a function to perform. It's only when we feel pain that we are alerted to a problem that needs our attention.

It's the same with grief. You need to allow yourself to feel the sorrow that is in your heart at the passing of so many things—the friends you may never see again, the place where you grew up, the local beauty spots where you picnicked, the pets you loved, the people who became special in your life. The loss of all these is to be keenly felt. It's no shame to find yourself six months later unexpectedly bursting into tears because of some poignant reminder.

As has been said earlier, tears of sadness are healthy for us because they chemically detoxify the body. It's unhealthy not to feel the pain and not cry. Don't let anyone tell you to "cheer up" or that you "mustn't cry." I remember being told by one well-meaning soul at my father's funeral, "Now then, don't cry." My dad was no more—I needed to cry.

Permission to Express Feelings

It's not enough to allow yourself to feel the pain; you need to express it. You must find ways of letting the pain out and letting the healing begin. The problem can be finding an acceptable way of expressing it and someone who can handle the expression. Your parents may be so caught up in their own grief process that they cannot listen to you.

Expression can take various forms. One TCK after a lifetime of mobility said: "We all have to deal with grief sometime in our lives. Friendships are broken, relations destroyed because of situations beyond our control. Love is something to be cherished, to be held deep in our hearts. Sometimes it is almost unbearable to say goodbye, when I hold that person for what may be the very last time in my life. The grief I'm feeling in the pit of my heart comes out in the form of tears cascading from my eyes."

All emotions, including anger, can find outlets in physical ways—though preferably not in destructive ways! Some people do aggressive exercise on the sport's field, some attack housework vigorously, and some find relief in fighting for a cause.

Recognizing anger is not hard, but finding safe outlets is more difficult. Apart from violence, some TCKs rebel and do things deliberately to upset those they hold responsible, notably their parents. I have the diary of a young woman who went from life overseas with a Christian charity to life back at a British university. She resented the changes that life had foisted on her and started using drugs. She moved from hashish to LSD to Ecstasy and went deeper into the drug scene, ending up in a lifestyle of crime. The poetry she wrote during those "wilderness years" is very poignant. Here is an example:

Sitting stoned.
One sleeps
One study
What is going on in our minds?
Why this fill of paranoia?
The distant callings lead me away
Mind wanders
To forests and jungles
Lost and forever searching
What is beyond
The unknown.
Is this the challenge?
What's the point in being here?
All it is is writing poetry and
Sitting stoned.

("Sitting Stoned")

This young woman made her way back to a new life by re-embracing her faith and finding that God welcomed her into his embrace; but not every one does so.

Pouring your heart out by keeping a journal, writing poetry, or writing to TCK friends you have known can be helpful in unloading how you are feeling. Your anger may not just be directed at what you are experiencing. It can also be directed at the injustice and inequality that hits you upon your return to the materialism of your own culture, if you are returning from the third world.

A teenager who had grown up in Thailand said: "The behavior of my peers annoyed me for years. I remember quite how immature they were and that they had experienced absolutely nothing but thought they were so grand! But generally, I didn't understand the need to discuss clothes, boys, makeup, sex, and other people, which happened all the time."

Someone who rants against social injustice and hypocrisy can appear very arrogant and self-righteous. How you express indignation is crucial in determining how you are accepted by your monocultural peers. Most young people in the West these days are acutely aware of environmental and social justice issues and want to do something about them. Equally, many live hedonistic lives, living for the pleasure of today with no thought for tomorrow. To many TCKs western youth appear shallow. But to criticize their lifestyles and compare their circumstances with those you left will not make you popular. You need to find friends who share your sense of justice and equity and engage their sympathy by sharing concerns instead of condemning them for their ignorance.

Pathways to Saying Goodbye

Saying goodbye lends a sense of completeness to a move. How many times have you heard someone say that they regret bitterly not having the chance to say goodbye to someone they loved before that person died? It's the same with saying goodbye to a former life, to the places, the people, and the pets. As mentioned in Part I, Dave Pollock has helpfully put this together as the RAFT experience.

R: Reconciliation. This means putting things right
before you leave a place. Don't leave with a bad
taste in your mouth. If you've had a disagreement
with someone, take or make the opportunity to go
and sort it out. You may never see them again, but
that doesn't matter. If you've tried your best to set
the record straight by apologizing or trying to heal
the breach, then your conscience is clear. You can
leave the hurt and the bitterness in the past. "Be
sure to say goodbye properly and not leave issues
hanging," advised one sixteen-year-old.

A: Affirmation. This means saying what was good
about the experience, putting together all the posi-
tives. For many TCKs this is the easy part. They
loved where they lived and didn't want to leave.
Everything about it seems better than what lies
on the other side. But there may have been bad or
hard parts also, and it is important to acknowledge
that. Even in difficult things, there is something
to learn. Affirmation prevents the farewell from
becoming a funeral.

F: Farewell. This means saying goodbye in
culturally appropriate ways to all the important
things and people in your life. One TCK who came
back at age nine said to me: "My biggest sadness
was not saying goodbye to our cats and where we
lived, since I was taken directly from boarding

school to England." If possible, ask your parents to give you the time and opportunity to visit all those people and places that you will miss.

Many TCKs found it helpful to return to the place where they grew up. Somehow, revisiting the significant places in their childhood and remembering their associations gives a sense of completion. My daughter-in-law and her sister went with their husbands back to Thailand where they grew up. There they were able to say goodbyes they had never said and to include their husbands in what was a very important part of their life history.

T: Think Destination. This means taking a realistic look at what life will be when you return. You need to anticipate the challenges you will face and the differences you will find. Knowing about yourself as a TCK helps, but so does being realistic about the skills and resources you will need to survive. It means building a network of people and agencies to which you can turn for help when you are charting your way through these unfamiliar waters.

People to Share Experiences

Says one TCK from Switzerland: "Get to meet other TCKs or at least cosmopolitan people very quickly and ignore anyone who tries to put down your experiences abroad."

If you're going to express pain, grief, and anger, then you will need to find a safe place in which to do it and a safe person with whom to share it. You need someone who is prepared to listen and not judge you, someone who will not be quick to offer advice or tell you how you should feel, someone who understands *why* you feel as you do. As I've already said, this is unlikely to be someone in your own family, though the family may go through grieving times together. By far, the best solution is someone who has been a TCK or, at the very least, lived overseas or spent considerable time with global nomads like yourself. "Find a good friend who understands (another TCK is best) and make sure you can trust him or her," advised one TCK who had lived in Egypt, Jordan, France, and Cyprus.

Besides emotions, you need to unpack your experiences, and most people have a concentration span of about five minutes when it comes to hearing other people's stories. One TCK on re-entering the United States said: "When I try to explain it to the 'folks back home' their eyes glaze over and they soon tire of the subject."

What's more, if you are trying to make new friends, be careful with your story telling. Many people are competitive when it comes to having a good story to tell: "I broke my leg climbing a tree." "Well, I got Tom Cruise's autograph." But a kid who's lived in the jungle, gone shark fishing and scuba diving every week, done their daily shopping in Manila, gone to school within sight of Mount Everest, or eaten grilled snake will have tales to tell that no one can better—and that's no fun at all!

All the TCKs I talked to stressed the importance of keeping links with the people they shared their lives with. They advised:

"Try and keep really good contact with your friends," and "Make sure you get addresses of all your friends."

Don't dwell on negative thoughts. Cherish the rich experiences you enjoyed and treasure the memories. At one camp for returning TCKs, I had each of the eight teenagers there bring a memory bag of things that were special to them from their time overseas. I allowed just over an hour for the session, and over two hours later, we were still talking. Finally, each had found others who were interested in their yearbooks, the photos of where they had lived, the significant people in their lives, and the strange and trivial mementoes they brought, each of which carried a special memory.

Finally, here's one piece of advice from someone who now works with TCKs to help them make the journey back: "Remember that the United Kingdom (or wherever) doesn't have to be home straight away. It can *become* home in time."

A professional windsurfer needs custom boards for wave sailing, because there are so many different places with a myriad of varying conditions. Wind speed and direction always differ. As you get better you develop preferences not only for the design but also for the way you like to set it up depending on your size and your sailing style. (*The Ultimate Guide to Windsurfing*, page 26)

— 8 —
NUTS AND BOLTS

"Don't be too gullible. When people tell you things, look at whom it is coming from. They can help you learn the slang and top ten chart songs without making you feel like a jerk."

That advice came from a TCK who was twelve when she re-entered. There's so much that's different when you come back and so much you just don't know or understand. As one TCK put it, "You feel like a real nerd!" One of the problems is that you know so much more than they do about all sorts of things, but you don't know anything about the things that matter to *them*.

What you need is a culture guide—someone who knows his or her way around and is prepared to steer you through the maze. That person needs to be someone you trust; someone who will be sensitive to your feelings and needs, who won't degrade you for asking dumb questions, and who has patience and time for you. However, you too need to retain a sense of proportion and laugh at yourself when you do or say something stupid.

It's ideal if you can arrange this mentoring relationship before you come home. Try as a family to find friends back home with kids of a similar age to you so you can begin building relationships of trust and respect. If you have already spent time with them during vacations or on leave, then these friendships should go more smoothly.

On the other hand, if you're coming back to college, you'll probably be in a place where you don't know anyone. In that case, take time to find someone who is sensitive to your needs. There may be a department that runs activities for international students, and you might fit in there better. At least, the people running it may have an awareness of living overseas, and it probably wouldn't take long in that environment to find another TCK from some walk of life.

There are plenty of places you can find help. If you are at college, there will be student counsellors; schools will have personal tutors; your local youth group or club will be a good place to make friends of your own age and find someone to show you around; check the student websites—and especially those set up for TCKs. Now let's look at some of the practical, down-to-earth issues you need to know as a returning TCK.

HOW TO FIT IN

When you're on the "outside," desperate to be part of the "in crowd," how do you do it? Just think of all the areas you want or need to know about if you're going to be part of your peer group.

What Do People Wear?

One TCK said: "It helped getting someone with enough tact and wisdom to make sure I was dressed 'right.' Mum tried before I went off to school, but I was eleven and awkward, and she only had two weeks in the country to get it all sorted, so she was not really up with what people were wearing."

How Do People Date?

If you are interested in someone, how do you show it? What's expected on the first date? Who's expected to pay? What if your partner is more sexually assertive than you are comfortable with? How do you say "no" and mean it? What are the dangers of sexual promiscuity?

What Do People Do for Leisure?

Do they go bowling, rollerblading, dancing, or something else? Are there skills you need to learn in order to take part? Which sports are popular? Which team should you support?

What about Music?

One TCK said: "My Dad made sure I listened to the top ten on World Service, and my friend did the same with CNN." Another commented: "Popular-culture changes are often very difficult to deal with. For example, music questions about nineteenth-century music are similar in all countries with a Western tradition. In contrast, the popularity of pop groups is very different in different countries. This led to some strange discussions, as the common ground was 'high culture,' which isn't necessarily a good thing if you are fifteen!"

What about Driving?

Can people your age drive? How many of them have cars? At what age can you learn to drive? If you have a license from somewhere else, can you exchange it? Are there restrictions on drivers under a certain age?

What about Drugs?

A TCK who is lonely is vulnerable, and drugs can seem like an easy escape from the loneliness. What do you do if you are offered drugs? Do you know what harm they can do to your health? How do you know when experimentation has become addiction? Where can you go for help if you get involved with drugs? Do you know the common street names for drugs? Most drug habits are funded by criminal activities. Do you know what the penalties are for drug use, drug pushing, and theft?

What about Smoking?

Smoking is banned in a lot of public places, but increasing numbers of young people smoke, since it is socially acceptable. Do you know enough to make a choice about this? Do you know the health risks? Do you know about passive smoking—the risks of being too long in a smoke-filled environment?

What about Alcohol?

Do you know the age at which drinking is legal in public places? Do you know the relative strengths of alcoholic drinks? How much can you safely drink and remain in control? Is it legal to drink and drive? If so, how much is permissible?

FINANCES, FEASTS, AND PHONES

Handling personal finances is a major issue for everyone leaving home. However, if you have come from a place where you had a very different standard of living, you may find it difficult to make the necessary adjustments. You may have come from an affluent expatriate lifestyle where you had live-in maids and money went a long way. It may be that you never had to be careful about your spending habits. Or, you may have come from a situation where you had or needed relatively little money to live. Suddenly, you are faced with an overwhelming array of goods and services—clothes, shoes, computers, eating out, and cell phones—that are expensive and that everyone says are *necessary*. How do you cope?

Finances

It is important to be realistic with regard to finances. You *can* get everything you want—but at a price. And, usually, that price is debt. I know of TCKs who got themselves into trouble in order to pay for the designer gear they felt they had to have. If you are still at home, discuss with your parents a reasonable allowance for them to give you—if they are able to give you one at all. This amount should be reasonable in view of what your parents earn and reasonable compared to what others get. Be warned: most young people get less allowance than they usually want to admit.

If you are going away to college, find out how much it costs just to live there. The cost of housing and the cost of living can vary greatly from region to region. This may be something to consider when choosing your place of study. Many students are choosing to live within commuting distance of home to save money, which may be economical but deprives them of the benefits of living in community with other students.

You also need to factor into your budget such things as the cost of books, paper, food, gifts, phone bills, and Internet expenses. Are there organizations you want to join? Do you plan to travel during the holidays? How much will those things cost?

Once you have done this research, figure out where the money will come from. Most students take out student loans, and they do get large amounts of money that way. But what are the implications of future debt repayment? What is the repayment schedule and at what rate of interest? Scholarships are available to some students. Take time to find out where, for which subjects, the criteria to qualify, and the deadlines for applications. In some parts of Europe, students are still paid to study, but that is becoming rare. In many parts of the world, the expectation is that you will work your way through college.

The next step is to work out a budget—one that balances. Start with an ideal goal of expenditures and then write down your income. If the two don't match, which is highly probable, then start working through the expenditures, cutting out things you really don't need.

Finding a Job. One way of easing the financial situation is to get some sort of part-time employment. Do you know what you need to have in order to get a job? Do you have a social security number? If you have always lived overseas, your parents may never have registered you into the system, and that can take time. Do you have some form of identity? Is there a national card you need? What are the restrictions on people of your age working? What skills do you have that would make you attractive to employers? Can you get a job on campus? Are your language and cross-cultural skills a particular asset here?

Many young people take Saturday jobs or employment after school to supply their needs. Large stores have fairly flexible work hours, give good training, and offer pleasant working conditions. There is less exploitation of young people nowadays, but there are still employers who hire young people who are desperate for money, at less than the minimum wage.

Most students help fund themselves through college by working either during the semester or during their vacations. Students should check with their school authorities regarding whether this is permitted. Some schools in Europe still forbid employment during the college semester. If you plan to get a vacation job, you need to apply early, particularly if you are staying in your college town. There are usually more students than there are jobs. One thing you may have that others don't is fluency in a second language. This may help you get a job during the tourist season.

If you do get a job, be sure to check on your tax status. In certain countries, if you earn under a certain amount, you do not need to pay tax. If you get an emergency tax coding because this is the first time you have worked, make sure you contact your employer to get it changed. And remember to reclaim the overpaid tax. Much of this will be up to you. The government will not necessarily take steps to see that you get what you deserve.

Ways to Save Money. Tear up your credit card or promise yourself to pay the balance in full each month. Interest on credit cards is horrendous. Some banks allow overdrafts to students, but remember you'll have to pay it back sometime. Buy in bulk with friends. Even if you have to use a cab once a month to carry all the groceries, it can still be cheaper. Buy store brands rather than recognized brands. Use coupons from the newspaper or fliers that come in the mail. Make a sack lunch instead of eating at the college bar. Shop at charity stores for clothes. It's smart; it's cheap; and you can get some really cool things. Moreover, you can develop your own personal style, something that is distinctly you and not part of the mass-production line. Walk or bike rather than using public transportation. Look into student discounts on transportation. Keep a separate bank account for money you are given for your birthday or Christmas, so you have a fund to occasionally buy yourself something special.

Banking. You need to get a bank account to pay your loans or grants and to get a checkbook and ATM card. At the beginning of the academic year, banks pursue student customers who they hope will stay with them for life. Check out which banks offer the best deal. Some will have vouchers for CDs or clothes, but the best deals are usually those offering to start you off with money in the bank. That way you decide what to spend it on. If you are unfamiliar with the banking system's cash machines, ATMs, and PIN (personal identification number), ask your mentor for explanations. You don't want to be the person with money in the bank who doesn't know how to get it out!

Feasts

When it comes to going out, how much should you expect to pay? Are guys still expected to pay when on a date? How do you get the best deals on meals? Watch for special offers for students on certain nights or between certain times. A lot of places make money on drinks, so the food is cheap. If you limit your intake of brand-name soft and alcoholic drinks, you can eat relatively cheaply. You can make drinks go further by asking for tap water with your meal, which should cost nothing. If you just ask for water, you might get bottled water, for which they will charge you. Take-out food is not always a cheap way of eating.

If you have never cooked for yourself, get a good, basic cookbook, something like *The Essential Student Cookbook* or *Cooking Outside the Pizza Box*.[1] And find out what are cheap and nutritious foods. Pasta, eggs, and cheese make good starters for the pantry. Besides buying in bulk and finding the supermarket with the best bargains, look for local markets. These will generally have cheap fruits and vegetables and, depending on where you have come from, they may have a flavor of home.

Phones

Almost everyone has a cell phone these days, but how do you get the best deal? Again, your guide or a friend of the family should be able to help you with this. One thing to take into consideration is what network your friends are on. It's no use getting a good deal with one network only to find that your friends are on another, because then it will cost a lot to call them. Ask around before making a decision. If you are going to college, you may want to do all the preliminary investigations but not buy a phone until you get there.

Cell phones are a common object of theft, particularly at bars or eating places. It takes only a moment for someone to remove a phone that has been placed on the edge of a table or on the floor. So, you constantly need to be security conscious. And be aware of what to do if it does get stolen: what is your liability, and how do you get a new one or stop someone using your old one? Similarly, if your credit card or checkbook gets stolen, do you know what number to call in order to prevent someone else from using it?

LEARNING THE LANGUAGE

A nurse who returned to the United Kingdom said: "I still say and do things that are culturally inappropriate. This tends to make my husband groan. But, at the moment, I have a very good American friend here, and it makes her laugh and feel less alien in the U.K."

Most TCKs would say that the biggest stumbling block to getting accepted is language, because language is a key to so much else. How we think, our worldview, and our approval or disapproval of things are all tied up, not just in what we say, but *how* we say it.

A North American TCK whose expatriate environment had been mainly British remarked: "It was strange to get blank stares when I used expressions and phrases in British and African English that were common in the multilingual environment like my school in Africa. Subsequently, I found out that people who are used to European English experience a similar thing."

Another North American TCK visiting the United Kingdom commented: "I kept calling trousers 'pants' when I first visited the U.K. I got some strange looks from ladies who assumed I could see their underwear."

After ten years in the jungle in Thailand, one girl noticed:

When we first got back, we found cars were very quiet—you couldn't hear them! I remember going down a hill and saying something along the lines of, "Boy, that's really neat!" My big sister turned round from the front seat and told me never to say things like that in this country. I can't ever remember saying it again.

My feeling was one of total alienation. It was a strange place, strange people, strange language, and it seemed strange to use English rather than Thai to communicate. I was totally out of my depth and didn't have a clue what to say or do.

Everyone says you have to do a lot of listening and watching, but it helps if you have some forewarning. You may not want to use swear words, but it helps to know what they are and what they mean so that you can recognize them when you hear them. Looking blank or shocked immediately sets you apart. You don't have to approve of them, but you don't have to look foolish or ignorant.

Before you come back, get someone to send you a couple of magazines for people your age. That will give you insight into what young people are interested in and what they talk and think about. Better still, get them to send you something regularly while you are overseas so that you always keep up with what people your age are doing. One returning teen commented: "I did not know the language, that is, swear words, or the TV, music, and fashion. Not knowing kids' TV continued to be a problem into my later teens. My peers would talk about old shows, but I could not remember stuff I had never seen!"

Another source of information is the soap operas and sit-coms that appear regularly on all television channels. Those that are set in your "home" country are generally a good guide to how people perceive themselves, even if they are a little exaggerated. They are also an introduction to modern idioms and have themselves spawned new words into the national language. In England the phrase *gob smacked*, which means "astounded," was first used by a television soap opera character.

Sometimes, you can live a protected lifestyle overseas and not be street-smart when it comes to life in a materialistic society. There is nothing wrong in being naive or innocent, but it does make you vulnerable. Knowledge empowers you to be the person you want to be and to make choices about your language and lifestyle that are informed.

Humor is a feature of language that differs radically around the world. Get people to send you jokes by e-mail that inform you of a national sense of humor. And when you do make a mistake with language, be willing to laugh at yourself. It helps to develop a fairly thick skin so that you don't take offense when people poke fun at you. They are not necessarily being unkind—making fun of you is sometimes a sign that you've been accepted into the "in crowd."

CHOOSING THE RIGHT SCHOOL

You are unlikely to be returning to a school system that's a mirror image of the one you've left. Here are some typical comments made by individuals entering a new school system:

"Didn't particularly like it—not as free, hated having to wear a school uniform, couldn't speak the lingo, and had a funny accent."

"It's more lax and easier but demanded different ways of thinking through certain subjects. You need more analysis, more thinking through things instead of memorizing everything you know."

"It's better because the teachers are not worried about the facts—they just want you to understand. But it can be frustrating because they focus on different things."

"The school here is a lot bigger. The social atmosphere is very different. The children tend to be less respectful and less well-behaved. Bullying and drugs are more prominent."

"There are environmental differences like litter, spitting, and foul language. People misuse their rights and responsibilities."

"As a British citizen, it is better for me (my old school was American), but there is a lot more focus on exams."

Those comments identify several differences. Teaching methods may vary. In some parts of the world, schooling is done by rote learning, which means you are expected to memorize the material the teacher delivers and to repeat it when you do your assignments. This is particularly true in the East and in two-thirds world countries. In the West, you will more likely be asked for critical analysis of what you have learned.

Similarly, some school systems demand a lot of exam work while others depend mainly on course work. Many international schools follow a North American curriculum. If you are not from the United States, you need to know what standard you will be expected to have reached in your own national curriculum if you are to fit back in. Many schools overseas now offer the International Baccalaureate, which is widely accepted as a qualification for tertiary education.

School sizes and cultures vary. Some children overseas attend schools with very small class sizes, as few as ten students or less. If you come back to an inner-city school, the class might be as much as four times that size. One TCK said: "I was no longer a 'somebody.' I was now a 'nobody.'"

If you have been part of a small school, the likelihood is that you will have been involved in pretty much everything that was going on. A sense of community develops in a small school, and people help each other out. There is more a culture of volunteering. One TCK I knew came from such a school to a huge comprehensive school. In his first year, he volunteered for anything that was going on—the school play, the football team, the orchestra—until he discovered that people just didn't do that sort of thing. It was definitely *not cool*. So he sat back and became withdrawn. He resented his previous experiences and his lack of preparation for this new way of life.

The dress code and code of conduct will be different too. You need to know acceptable ways of dressing and of behaving at school. Most schools have a written code of behavior, with clear indications of the penalties if you break that code.

Expectations

Generally, people only understand what they have experienced, and most people you meet will not have a clue what it was like going to school elsewhere. They will presume you had an inferior education, probably something along the same lines as they are getting, only much worse. Listen to these comments:

> "School was much worse, both as an academic and
> social experience, although my peers considered me
> to have naturally received a poor education because
> we were in Africa. I was even asked if we had
> pencils!"

"When I was in the top grade, we had someone come in to talk about the jungle, and he brought some slides with him to show everyone. It was the first time I really became aware that when I talked to my friends about Chefoo, they really had no concept of what jungle looked like. Afterwards everyone was asking me, generally in amazement, whether my school was really in that kind of environment."

"School is much worse. In Peru I went to a private school where all the rich kids went. The facilities for students there were abundant, such as advanced laptops instead of textbooks, music rooms, and lots of sport facilities like courts, pool, and an indoor stadium."

"Telling others you are bilingual is definitively *not* on! 'Say something in such and such a language' happens at least twenty times a day. News really travels fast at school."

"You need to sort out your expectations of school too. If you assume it will be worse, then it probably will be. Try to approach a new school with an open mind; be prepared for people not making allowances for you. If you look as though you belong, people will assume you know the way things work at school. After all, you've only changed schools, haven't you?"

"I was having a conversation with one person in a dinner queue in my first week at school. Turning around to continue the conversation after responding to a greeting, I got very confused when I could not tell whom I had been talking with. All white people wearing the same clothes looked the same!"

Making Choices

In the past you may not have had the opportunity to choose your school, since there may only have been one accessible to you. When you return, there may be several options, though not if you wait until the last minute to put in your application. If you know you are coming home to school, get friends to find out what possibilities are open to you and what you need to do to apply. Sometimes that is difficult if you don't know exactly where you will be living. Some schools within a town will have restricted enrollment, and you may not be able to attend the one you want to if you can't prove you live within the area. Others are overcrowded; if you don't get your name down early, you will not get in.

Similarly, choosing what subjects you will study can be tricky if you have not had the opportunity to study some of the subjects offered at your current school. Many TCKs choose subjects from a narrow list and then wish they had chosen something different, something about which they had no previous experience. Others choose a subject because it is different, but they may do so without researching what it really entails.

The same goes for choosing higher education courses. There is an enormous choice of subjects, and, if your current school does not have a career counselor, you may not know what qualification a particular course of study will give you. Because TCKs often find it hard to look far down the road, they do not always make good career choices. You need to ask the question, "If I follow this path of study, what possibilities does it open for me three to five years from now?"

Universities and colleges have different ways of teaching and different types of campuses. Some are in the middle of cities and some out in the country. Some have live-in accommodations; at others you are expected to find your own. Can you make these choices without having made a visit to the location?

There are a hundred other practical things you may need to know before settling down into your new country. Here are some words of advice from TCKs themselves:

- Learn to use a launderette or washing machine and an iron.

- Learn to use a cooker or microwave.

- Learn to use electrical equipment, such as kettles, toasters, sandwich-makers, lawnmowers, photocopiers. Don't be afraid to ask how it works before you try to use it.

- Learn good study habits and how to use a public library.

- In the first few months at school, do more observing than talking.

- Let others know that in the country you have come from things are done differently, and be honest in

telling them that you are not used to doing things
their way.

- Don't panic if you're having a problem.
- Be friendly and sociable. Don't isolate yourself.
- Get involved in sports. Attend social functions.
- Learn to get the most out of your money by investing
  and saving.
- No question is too dumb so don't be afraid to ask.

STAMPING OUT WORRY

Making the transition back to your country of passport can
be an anxious time because of changes in lifestyle, climate, language, customs, and expectations. With a little forethought, you
can develop some strategies to cope with your natural anxieties.
Here are some suggestions you might follow before you do something new.

Clarify Exactly What You Are Worried About

Often when we are worried, our thoughts are not very clear.
Try to figure out exactly what you are worried about. It might
help to write it down, or write a list of your top five worries. It
can help to bring it out into the open: I'm worried that when I
start school, I won't make friends. What will I do at lunch time if
I have no friends?

Be a Detective

What is the evidence that what worries you is likely to happen? Don't assume you're right; instead, write a list of evidence for and against: I might not make friends, but out of a class of thirty people, I'll probably find someone I like.

Plan for the Worst Outcome

If your worries are right (which they might not be), think up a plan to make things easier: I could take a book with me so that I have something to do during that first lunchtime, if I'm lonely.

Put Yourself in Someone Else's Shoes

What advice would you give to someone with your concerns? What advice might your friends give if you asked them? They say things like this: All you can do is your best and be yourself. Why wouldn't they like you? You've had friends before and you will again, even if it takes time. It's better to go and try than to continue worrying.

Stop Thinking in Black and White

Usually things aren't all good or all bad, not a complete success or a complete failure. Remind yourself that things are usually in between. It will take some time to settle into your new situation. You can tell yourself: Okay, I might not be popular with everyone, but I'll probably make some new friends. I might enjoy it; it might be nothing at all like I'm dreading.

Give Yourself "Worry Time"

Give yourself fifteen minutes a day to worry and try to solve your problems or the ones you think you have. If you find yourself worried at other times, tell yourself to postpone this type of thinking until your official "worry time."

Keep Perspective

Try to worry only about the things that are really important. Think positively. Try to relax and take one step at a time. Will this matter to you in ten years? This is the start of something new—an adventure. Maybe it's more important to take your time and make good friends who will last.

Learn to Listen

Is there anything you can do to stop yourself from worrying? Can you do anything to change the situation? Planning your first day at school might help. Although it's tempting to talk about where you are from, it's important to listen as well. Find out about other people's lives and how things work in your new situation.

Distract Yourself

If there is nothing you can do now, find something to take your mind off whatever is worrying you. Some typical distractions are watching television, playing sports or music, and talking to people you know and are comfortable with. But don't be afraid to tell someone what is worrying you. They can't help unless you tell them. And remind yourself each day of the progress you are making.

HELPFUL TCK WEBSITES

www.tckworld.com—website for TCKs everywhere founded by Dr Ruth Useem who coined the phrase "Third Culture Kid." This website contains her research together with many links to other TCK resources.

www.transition-dynamics.com—an independent consultancy serving the international expatriate community.

www.figt.org—Families in Global Transition provides strategic resources for those who live and move about the world.

www.gnvv.org—a website maintained by Global Nomads International contains a number of links.

www.overseasbrats.com—an organization for those associated with American schools overseas.

www.sietart.org—Society for Intercultural Education, Training and Research runs an annual conference on aspects of international relocation.

www.xenosmk.org—a British-based organization for TCKs, activities and articles.

www.mkplanet.com—mkPLANET is a growing community designed and run by current missionary kids (MKs) and adult missionary kids (AMKs) providing information, interaction, and support on MK/TCK-related issues.

> There are two basic rules: 1) Never go out alone, and 2) Stay close to shore within the break, then if you do have a problem, you can bodysurf back to shore. (*The Ultimate Guide to Windsurfing*, page 68)

— 9 —

THE THIRD CULTURE COMMUNITY

We had the experience; we missed the meaning.

(T. S. Eliot, "The Dry Salvages")[1]

The experience of re-entry is a voyage of self-discovery. Most of us assume that our current lives are normal, and if we did return to the land of our mother tongue, we would easily fit in and understand the culture. So it comes as a severe shock when we do return and not only cannot read the signs linguistically, literally, or culturally, but also we are constantly being misread ourselves. Most returning TCKs find it challenging to fit in, and some have felt like "an alien," "a peculiar beast," and "a rare specimen."

One thing that can help you come to terms with this is realizing you are not on your own but are part of a global Third Culture

Kid community. How you feel about yourself, your environment, your friends, and your family is the same way thousands of others like you feel. It would be strange if you did *not* feel that way.

Knowledge is empowering. If you know that the symptoms you are experiencing—loneliness, alienation, depression, grief, despair, frustration—are a normal part of going through transition, then you can begin to accept your emotions and deal with them one by one. Transition, change, moving from one place to another, from one stage of life to another is a process, and a process always takes time. Just as it takes time to recover from an illness, it takes time to recover from a move.

Be aware of your own feelings and stress reactions. What do you usually do when things bother you? Do you withdraw into yourself and hide from the world? Do you go out and blow the stress away? Watch out for the danger signals that mean you are not just experiencing the normal reaction to change but have begun a dangerous spiral toward clinical depression or suicidal thoughts. Find someone to talk to before it gets serious. The longer you stay cooped up in your room, the less likely you are to seek help, and the worse it will get.

It is important to recognise the danger signals that what may be a problem is descending into a serious issue which needs professional help. Anger and bitterness are often experienced but if they are not brought out into the open they can have devastating consequences—broken and unhealthy relationships, delayed adolescent rebellion in the 20s and 30s, and an inability to commit. Look for the danger signs—cynicism, chronic negativity, depression, uncontrolled habits, escapism, withdrawal, overreaction to small events, and negative responses to authority. Similarly, a lack of control over their lives has led some TCKs into eating disorders, their diet being the one thing they can control. Watch out for initial lack of appetite turning into anorexia. Be aware of when loneliness and difficulty in forming new relationships descends into a depression, which goes beyond mere sadness and leads you to entertain suicidal thoughts. Recognise any signs of compulsive and obsessive behavior, resisting connectivity, lack of trust, and overreaction. Beware of cults, which hold out the attraction of being a "special person."

Besides realizing you are part of a global Third Culture Kid community, a second way of coming to terms with being a TCK is to find others who share that experience and who will help see you through it. Time and again, TCKs advised returning TCKs to talk through how they feel with another TCK. It may be that someone within your parents' organization is already back, and you can be put in touch with them. Or you may have kept in contact with someone who left a year or two before you. Wherever you are, seek them out.

With another TCK, you can compare notes on your adjustment. Find out how long it took them to feel settled. Some would say they have never really felt settled; others find their feet within a year; others take longer. If you realize you are not a special case, then you cease to act like one and stop feeling sorry for yourself. Someone who has been through the experience will have a different perspective on it.

CITIZENS OF THE WORLD

Living overseas gives you a unique outlook on the world and its peoples. But when you return home, you need to realize that most people will not share that perspective. So you need to be as patient with them as you expect them to be with you. Just as you have a lot of dumb questions to ask about this culture you are entering, so they will have similar questions about the culture you left, such as: "You're not very brown if you've always lived in Africa, are you?" or "Do they have television in Papua New Guinea?" or "Are there streets full of wild animals in Nairobi?"

Let people ask questions and don't make them feel bad for asking. Take the opportunity to broaden their worldview without preaching to them. One thing your experience of making and losing so many friends should have taught you is how to take the initiative. It is said that when one TCK meets another, they have three questions: (1) What's your name? (2) Where are you from? and (3) How long are you staying?

In other words, *is it worth investing my time in this relationship?* Upon re-entry you will have the opportunity to make longer-lasting relationships. Since you know how to make friends quickly, you need to use this skill in your new environment. Don't wait for people to come to you; be prepared to take the initiative and make friends. To do this, just be yourself and watch for the cultural cues on how to talk to people. Many TCKs commented on the need to develop "small talk." This is the ability, when first meeting someone, to say very little but be very friendly and polite. In most social encounters, people exchange words on the most trivial of subjects, and you will be expected to do the same thing.

It's far too easy for TCKs to come across as overly critical of their present culture and its perceived shallowness. The best thing is to accept that this culture is different, not worse or better, just different. Do not constantly compare your passport country with what you feel is your home country. Don't be critical of luxurious living and what you believe to be hypocrisy. Instead, look for contributions you can make. You can retain the integrity of your values without criticizing those of others. Be flexible and good-humored during this passage of transition.

One of the best ways of making friends is to take an interest in other people's lives and stories. Don't expect everyone to be excited about your life and experiences as a TCK—they won't always be. But if you start to ask them questions and get them talking, then they will more than likely return the compliment. One TCK said: "Be 100 percent where you are. Don't live in the past. Accept others as they are, just as you did in your overseas community."

There may be ways in which you can put your "world-citizen experience" to good use. One is with international students who come to study in your country. You understand some of the things they are going through and can empathize with them. Most colleges have some sort of support program for such students, and you may find it helpful to get involved. Another is to be involved with helping plan student travel or getting involved in short-term overseas programs or vacations organized by your school, church, or community.

BRIDGING THE GAP

Because you are part of this worldwide community of TCKs, you will draw strength and support from those you left behind. It is important not to block out the past. Many TCKs spoke of the need to recognize that the past is just that—past. It is important not to live in the past or to dwell too long on it. But you have probably left a piece of your heart in that place and with those people. Retaining contact by phone, e-mail, or letter is important in building bridges between your two worlds. In the film *My Big Fat Greek Wedding,* a must-see for those who have lived cross-culturally, the advice is given: "Don't let your past dictate who you are. Let it become part of who you will be."

Since your old friends are outside of your current situation, you may find it helpful to share with them how you are feeling. One TCK put it this way:

> Leaving my old friends behind was very hard. It is strange but right before and after you leave them, the bonds between you get stronger. When you have a problem, you want their advice first and you are more willing to listen to their advice. I am not very good at writing e-mails, but when I write to them, I am a lot more honest than I would ever be to anyone else. I guess it's just knowing that there is someone out there who knows you and is thinking of you. You feel like you have left a little bit of yourself with them and like you are carrying a bit of their heart.

Once you have been back for a little while, you may find it helpful, even therapeutic, to revisit the places that were an important part of your early life. For some, this is not possible because those places either no longer exist or are closed to tourists. If it is possible to raise the finances and arrange a trip, take time to go to all those places that hold special meaning and significance: the place where you spent your holidays, your school, and your neighborhood. One TCK who had grown up in Uganda said: "When it rains hard, I hear rain on an African tin roof, and I cherish the memory."

In the meantime, try to take one day at a time, focus on the now, and try not to worry about everything all at once. Give yourself time to have all the different feelings. Most of all, be your own best friend. Look after yourself and treat yourself to nice things from time to time to cheer yourself up.

THE VOYAGE OF SELF-DISCOVERY

At the beginning of this section of the book, we looked at what it means to be a TCK. As you go through transition and adjustment, you find out what it means to be you. A TCK who returned for college said: "I was finding out who I was and what I wanted to do."

Another whose parents had been teachers in Papua New Guinea, where she did all her schooling, said about choosing her life partner: "I was looking for someone who valued my past. When I took him back to Papua New Guinea, he became part of me."

You learn to be thankful for being a TCK without always needing to broadcast it. Self-discovery means accepting who you are without resenting the process. There will be pain that you have to accept and hurts for which you need to forgive someone. You cannot rewrite the past, but you can influence what it does to you. You can become a victim or an agent of change.

Some of your hurts and grievances may make you a person who can help others in hurtful situations. We live in a fragmented society where people find it hard to build relationships that last. Many of you have come from community-based societies where people act for the good of the whole and are less self-centered. Modeling that sort of relationship can benefit others.

You may have to rebuild your place within the family, both nuclear and extended. Most young people have to redraw the family picture after they leave home. This can play a larger part for TCKs. If a sense of feeling whole has always come from a relationship with your parents, the process of leaving them and making new, lasting relationships can be very painful and difficult, especially when you choose your life partner. At that point, you have to come to terms with making a fresh start with someone who will be more important and crucial to your security and well-being than your parents have been. A new form of dependence, or rather interdependence, has to develop.

Because some TCKs feel they have been marginalized by their parents in decision-making, the relationship may have to be rebuilt. There needs to be honest talking and a willingness to ask for, and to grant, forgiveness on both sides. It is sad to meet TCKs who have let the pain of past hurts sour not only their relationships with their parents but also with their own children. Parents are sometimes made to pay for hurts they unwittingly inflicted on their children by being denied access to their grandchildren or by having strict boundaries placed on their spheres of influence.

Discovering who you are involves revisiting the past, accepting it, and working through its consequences. But there then needs to be a willingness to move on. For some TCKs there is, at this point, a need to seek professional counseling. If so, it is best if you can find someone with an overseas perspective who will understand what is normal in the transition process. They will then be able to discern where your particular problems are coming from.

QUESTIONS AND ANSWERS

It is often said that there are more questions than answers in life, and that will probably continue to be the case. Some of the most obvious questions we all have to answer are: Who am I? Where have I come from? What am I doing here? Where am I going? These are questions I hope this book has helped you to start asking. And I hope you have some idea of where to look for the answers.

Beyond those questions are all sorts of things you need to know as you start this new phase of your life. You need to find people who will support you through the process and direct you to find answers to such questions as: Who are the people you can expect to be on the receiving end when you return? Are your parents going to be around, or are they just bringing you home and returning overseas? If they will not be there, then who can you turn to and rely on? How good are your contacts with your relatives? Do you know them well enough to make them a home-base? If they can't offer you a home away from home, who could give you space for your belongings and a bed for vacations or weekend visits?

Who do you call if you get into trouble? Who will offer you unconditional love and support? Initially, whom do you go to in an emergency? Do you know the telephone numbers for the emergency services? If you are at college, find out the student-support services that are available. For example, are there counseling services for such circumstances as rape, drug addiction, debt, or relationship difficulties? Make sure you know how to get help before you need it.

Who will be your culture guide or mentor? You need some-one roughly your age. This is someone who will take you to the local hot spots and show you how things work. This is someone who will kindly answer your dumb questions and will not laugh in your face or remind you in public of just how ignorant you were when you arrived. This needs to be a relationship of trust.

Remember, there is no such thing as a dumb question. Too many TCKs have ended up in some kind of trouble because they didn't have the courage to ask the right questions or know the right person to ask.

As a Third Culture Kid you have an enormous range of skills and experiences to draw on as you enter the world of study and employment. Recognize those abilities and learn from those ex-periences in order to avail yourselves of all the opportunities they afford. Don't deny your Third Culture; instead, delight in it. Just because you feel and, indeed, are different from your monocul-tural peers, this does not mean you have to deny your identity. Take time to discover what that identity is and affirm it. There's no safer place to conduct such a discovery than within the bounds of the Third Culture community. Make the effort to find out what facilities there are for meeting other TCKs upon your return or on your school campus.

And the final advice from TCKs on how to help them adjust to their new life:

1. Don't treat me like a celebrity, just let me be normal

2. Pursue me as a friend quickly

3. Let me watch for a while before expecting me to participate

4. Let me be a kid

5. Let me ask questions

6. Show me around and take me to youth activities

7. Help me fit in by telling me about music and fashions

8. Introduce me to your friends

9. Tell me when I get it wrong

10. Accept I might be different

Remember: No one understands a TCK better than another TCK.

Part III

ON THE
RECEIVING END

INTRODUCTION

As has already been shown, coming back to the country of passport is often the most difficult part of expatriates' careers, whether they are young or old. Too much of their sense of identity, belonging, and role is tied with other people and other places. Inevitably, leaving produces a sense of loss and grief, even if the situation was difficult or dangerous.

Those who had positive re-entry experiences highlighted the significant part played by those who were there to receive them. Effective, caring support systems can ease transition as well as provide the time and space for personal reflection and rehabilitation.

To enable this to happen, those receiving the returnee not only need to understand clearly what is involved at practical and emotional levels, but they also need the ability to empathize with the issues being faced. The following chapter highlights these issues and suggests ways of implementing procedures to make a positive difference.

The last chapter says to the Christian community, many who go overseas with a sense of God's call, that He has a purpose for them to fulfill outside of their passport cultural identity. For them, there are bigger questions to be faced upon return, especially if the experience has not turned out as anticipated. They will have questions about the guidance and the sovereignty of God, questions about obedience and right choices, and questions such as, What will my sending church think?

Because Christian service should be conducted within the community of believers, whatever form of expression that community may take, it is right that all those who are part of the community should share the experience of the home-comers and share the responsibility for their well-being.

In addition, I want to challenge the Christian community to rediscover what it means to be a pilgrim on this earth, to recognize, as Paul said, that our citizenship is in heaven (Philippians 3:20), and to learn to cling less tightly to material possessions and places. It is not just Christian workers overseas who are called to lead a nomadic existence and leave a place of belonging. In our hearts all of us who follow Jesus Christ are called to belong to him and to "seek first the kingdom of God" (Matthew 6:33). This is an exciting journey we share, a journey that calls for radical discipleship and a fresh expression of community. To complete the space analogy, we have the opportunity, like Captain Kirk of *Star Trek*, to "boldly go where no one has gone before!"

> What is a goodbye? It is an empty place in us. It is any situation in which there is some kind of loss, some incompleteness, when a space is created in us that cries out to be filled. Goodbyes are any of those times when we find ourselves without a someone or something that has given our life meaning and value, when a dimension of our life seems to be out of place or unfulfilled. Goodbyes are all of those experiences that leave us with a hollow feeling somewhere deep inside. (Joyce Rupp, *Praying Our Goodbyes*)[1]

— 10 —

THE RECEPTION COMMITTEE

Whether you are single, a family unit, or an older teenager returning for college education, one of the most vital ingredients in achieving a successful re-entry is the strength of support you receive on your return. Those who have shared a similar experience to your own will be best able to understand and support you emotionally through the time of readjustment. But there are plenty of others who can and should be involved. And, indeed, there are some who want to be involved but often don't understand what's going on.

This chapter is for them—the extended family, the local church, the neighborhood friends, the long-term supporters, and the sending agency. How can they be effectively involved in easing their friends, relatives, or cross-cultural worker back into society and the workplace? Hopefully, they will read the first nine chapters to understand the process of transition. This chapter is intended to give practical suggestions on what to do and how to do it.

There are several areas in which the returning expatriate needs solid, practical help or advice. Much of what is needed requires a little forethought to put systems or resources into place. So much of what we take for granted as a normal part of everyday life is alien to the returning expatriate. Life changes so quickly these days, technology progresses, and we absorb these changes without really registering them. Just think of the advances made in the last three years in technology, transportation, and the logistics of running a business, home, or career. Anyone who has spent only vacation time at home during that time may not have encountered those advances or been required to learn how to operate within those confines.

A WARM WELCOME

If you are coming home after a long absence far away, one of the nicest things is to be met at the airport by people who understand that you are tired, sad, confused, and wishing you were somewhere else. It is important that all those connected with the returnees communicate so that they don't show up at the same time and overwhelm the family. Who is actually going to drive them home? Where is home to be? The reception party might be armed with something to drink, something to distract the kids, and a readiness to do business with the airport staff in the eventuality of problems, such as a lost suitcase.

The welcome extends also to allowing the returnees some personal space. Appreciate their sense of loss and grief. Expect them to be fairly silent, moved by powerful emotions, and prone to expressions of grief and an inability to communicate effectively. The welcome may take the form of arranging some time off soon after arrival, away from everything and everybody that wants to consume them. Accept that they need time to regroup as a family, a couple, or an individual. Don't encourage them to take on too much too soon—just let them be. In the period of transition, there is a danger of acting simply for the sake of action. Too often firms, churches, and friends with the best of motives encourage returnees to participate and take up roles long before they are ready. This prevents them from working through the emotions, questions, and dilemmas they are facing.

A GOOD LISTENER

First and foremost returnees need friends who will listen to them. Many refer to the fact that no one was really interested in them or the lives they had been leading. Their self-worth may be challenged by a superficial welcome, which acknowledges their return but quickly moves on and ignores them. Returning cross-cultural workers who have regularly sent prayer letters back home discover that few people have really read them and retained any knowledge of the situation.

If you are part of the reception committee, make it your business to see that there is someone who can give time and empathy to the returnees and who will not give advice on how they *should* be feeling or what they *ought* to have done. People who have come from a small rural community in a two-thirds world country may feel threatened by their new situation and find it hard to function in large groups. Make sure there is a small group with whom they can relax and begin to take up the reins. Don't force them into big occasions.

A good listener demonstrates some appreciation of the situation. It is helpful if this person is someone who has had an overseas experience. If there is no one around in that category, then this person can always take time to learn about the place of service.

A good listener does not criticize. People on their return are very vulnerable, often ambivalent about the situation, fearful of making mistakes, and frequently feeling insignificant, purposeless, and insecure. All of these feelings need to be taken into consideration when listening to their stories. One person who returned with his wife and young family after a traumatic time in West Africa wrote the following to me:

> I have a great number of stories about my experiences overseas—many of which I would like to share simply for the catharsis of sharing the experience— but the vast majority are not very funny and only profoundly sad—too sad and overwhelming to tell easily. Who wants to hear about a dictatorial headmaster who regularly abused kids, told parents I was a saint, and fainted during staff meetings because he

was so drunk? Who wants to hear about my slinking past throngs of machine guns firing and demonstrating crowds to fetch my pre-school child on the other side of town? Who wants to know that I heard a kid being beaten to death but didn't do anything until it was too late? Who wants to know I was almost shot in my first week overseas as a missionary, or that someone tried to kidnap our child in the street, and my wife was followed and mugged three times in the first month? My supporters don't, and to be frank, I wouldn't either. And so, re-entry means publishing a life lived overseas and the pressures of public taste mean that it's prudent, necessary, but often, awkward to edit that life.

Someone needs to take responsibility for ensuring that each returnee, adult or child, has the opportunity to be properly de-briefed, both personally and professionally. Adequate funds should be set aside for that purpose.

PRACTICAL KNOWLEDGE

Setting up home, returning to the job market, and fulfilling legal requirements all take time and a working knowledge of the system. If you have been out of the bureaucratic loop for some years, it will take time and patience to get back in the process. One person who came home to retire after thirty years overseas said to me: "I came home to find that I had to get my electricity from the gas supplier, my phone from the television company, and my banking from the supermarket."

When you are bombarded with firms wanting to get your business, how do you decide which is best? It is difficult enough when you live in a settled situation; but, in the chaos and uncertainty of transition, decision-making is doubly difficult.

The reception committee should work out, on a need-to-know basis, what are the crucial things that the returning people will need within the first few weeks. Having someone who gathers the necessary forms to register for utilities, to enroll in the neighborhood schools, and to get credit rating from the banks is a blessing beyond belief. Much of this sort of help should be organized before the returnees arrive, if at all possible. Think creatively and strategically regarding what your returnees will require in order to function at a basic level on a day-to-day basis.

Paperwork is always a nightmare. What do they need to do to register for income tax? Do they need to renew their driver's license, or is there a limited period during which they can convert their overseas license to a domestic one? If there are young people going to college or university, there will be a mountain of paperwork to complete, and it needs to be filled in accurately to prevent delays. It helps to have someone who can do the research on such subjects and be on hand to help with the application process.

Practical advice can also extend to the "how-to-use" subjects. Much of this will have to do with technology. How do you choose which mobile phone to buy and the best plan? How do you use cash machines? What is broadband? How do you make purchases online? I recently recommended a book to a group of returning expatriates and said they could get it at Amazon.com. I might as well have been speaking Mandarin to some of them, because they were not used to having easy access to computers and the Internet. One TCK told me it took her two years to use a Coke machine because she didn't know how to work it and didn't want to appear dumb by asking. Her ignorance was discovered when a friend gave her some money and asked her to get a Coke from the machine down the hall. There was nothing to do but own up to her lack of knowledge.

SOCIAL AND CULTURAL ILLITERACY

Besides technological changes, the values of a society are constantly shifting. Making friends and reviving relationships is an exhausting business. Young people may find that dating customs and social networks are very different from what they are used to. Language also changes. Nuances alter, and words that were acceptable a few years ago may have taken on quite a different meaning. Expatriate communities often lag behind in their use of language. Often it is easy to spot expatriates by the dated terminology they use. A good friend who is spending personal time with a returnee might want to gently correct language usage.

Many who return have serious questions about the culture to which they are returning—and rightly so. Just because new values have been adopted or new norms accepted, doesn't mean that returnees will readily adopt them. However, sometimes returnees need a safe place to express their reservations and criticisms, so that they are not ostracized from the very people with whom they are trying to reintegrate.

Returnees often have a hard time socializing back into their passport culture. Cultural stress can provoke various reactions, as I have already stated. One way of dealing with this discomfort is to withdraw from society and avoid those situations where interaction is required with bothersome people and troubling mores. Helping returnees reintegrate socially and culturally often involves encouraging them to attend small gatherings and not accepting no for an answer. Watch for signs of depression and withdrawal. If your friend is not verbalizing difficulties, perhaps you might initiate conversation on the subject.

Some returnees turn to daydreaming, alcohol, or prolonged Internet use. Some lose their appetites or develop eating disorders. Some slide into clinical depression and become suicidal. If you have any cause for concern, make sure you know where your friend can turn for help. The subject becomes particularly important when it concerns the children of expatriates. Many children develop eating disorders or are tempted to self-harm. If the children are away at college, they need to know to whom they can go if these feelings overtake them.

Illiteracy will extend also to the world of music, books, and, most of all, television. In an age dominated by the lives of characters in television shows, ignorance about these celebrities marks a returnee apart as someone from another planet. Even if returnees are not interested in watching a lot of television or going to a lot of movies, they will hear these celebrities' names come up in conversation or on the news. For young people returning, the world of popular music needs to be understood. Again, these are areas where the good reception committee will have taken some action before the return, and, preferably, for the duration of the stay overseas. Sending magazines, videos, and tapes of what is current helps expatriates keep up-to-date. Of course, satellite television has helped open up the world to domestic productions, so staying culturally informed has never been easier.

PRACTICAL PROVISION

If you know your returnees really well, then you will know what practical provisions they will need in order to start over. First and foremost is housing. Do they have their own? If so, in what state of repair is it? Have the tenants left it clean? If they don't have their own home, is their company making provision for them? Do they have relatives who will keep them initially? Do they need to rent a place? If so, what size does it need to be, and what is the budget? I know of several churches that make it their business to provide accommodations for returning missionaries. They do the groundwork of finding a real estate agent to discover what properties are available and on what terms.

Once a house is located, there is the question of furnishings. If the returnees will need new things, what can you do to make sure there are adequate supplies to accommodate eating and sleeping? Many returnees have been overwhelmed by the generosity of their supporters when they find that the house they will live in, whether their own or rented, has been stocked with food and provisions. It does not need to cost a lot, and it is a practical gesture that means a great deal.

Sometimes the immediate need is transportation to the doctor, the dentist, the school, the stores, the local authorities, and the bank. Do you know anyone who has a car they could lend for the interim? Is there any charitable, short-term provision for transportation needs? Will the returnees need help choosing a car to buy?

What do they do about finding a doctor and dentist and getting health insurance? Did they have medical check-ups before they left the field? Is there an international health program that can give them thorough medical examinations? Have any members of the family developed illnesses while overseas for which they need immediate medical attention? Again, thinking through these issues *before* the return means that some action can be taken in advance of the needs.

FINANCIAL PROVISION

Some expatriates return with money saved from their overseas employment. Some voluntary workers find that the minute they set foot on shore, their support dries up since they are no longer perceived to be "on the front line" and, therefore, worthy of support. For many, the trip home means a considerable disparity in the cost of living and the availability of funds. Food, clothing, shelter, and even phone calls may all have been fairly cheap, even if basic. Most Western cultures have sophisticated lifestyles. Teenagers, particularly, struggle with the need for the right brands of shoes, jeans, and T-shirts. Expatriates feel alien enough without bearing the stigma of being dressed in yesterday's fashion. If you are part of a support network, think about getting together a budget to provide a basic wardrobe and someone to take returnees shopping where they get good value for their money.

Before the return, the expatriate needs a reminder of all these things so they can realistically think through what it is going to cost them to resettle. Where will their provision come from? Is the church, agency, or firm prepared to continue to give them an allowance to help them during the transition period? What about social security numbers and entitlements to benefits during the time they are seeking employment? What is required to set up a bank account? Many banks require special identification to handle any over-the-counter transactions. Is your returnee familiar with Internet banking?

ADVICE FROM RETURNING EXPATRIATES

The best advice in any situation comes from others who have been through a similar experience. The following list is culled from research questionnaires sent to expatriates. It is worth noting that much of the advice relates to communication and relationship skills.

- Be patient
- Listen
- Appreciate the sense of loss
- Make them feel loved and wanted
- Do things with them
- Be interested
- Ask questions
- Meet and talk
- Give them a chance to unload feelings
- Don't expect them to be "national"
- Understand transition
- Take them shopping
- Offer quiet places
- Give technical support and advice

- Ask what they need
- Help with budget and finance
- Be friendly
- Show encouragement to families

> The essential thing "in heaven and earth" is . . . that there should be a long obedience in the same direction; there thereby results, and has always resulted in the long run, something which has made life worth living. (Friedrich Nietzsche)[1]

— 11 —

THE PILGRIM COMMUNITY

Many people go overseas because of a sense of vocation, not just in the personal sense but in the sense that they felt the call of God on their lives and responded in obedience to that call. For them, "coming home" has many facets other than the practical and emotional aspects of making a transition. Some may be leaving after a lifetime of service that has drawn to a natural close, and they are now seeking guidance for the next phase of their lives.

Others, who come home because of an unexpected disruption to their service, whether that is bereavement in the family or a political upheaval, may struggle with the purpose of that disruption in the divine plan. Still others, who choose to come home because of children's educational needs or changes in personal circumstances, may be forced to deal with searching questions from those around them.

Churches, sending agencies, and supporters do not always demonstrate compassion and a willingness to understand the dilemma and trauma that returning cross-cultural workers face. Those who looked forward to being received back into the bosom of their Christian family frequently face disappointment and disillusionment when they are met with blank stares or questions such as, "Are you new here?" Returnees may also feel frustrated when others fail to comprehend the reasons for their return or be ignorant about the difficulties of re-entry.

Most of this book has addressed expatriates facing the return "home." I hope it has been helpful across a wide spectrum of people and situations. It is good to acknowledge this commonality and to affirm the normality of this experience. However, these issues are not unique to the missions community. Because we are humans created in the image of a God who knows joys and sorrows, we all feel the joys and sorrows of meetings and partings.

I want to address those faith issues the Christian community faces when a mission worker, one sent out by Christ and the church, returns to the country of origin. It is inappropriate for Christians to think of these transitions as "suffering for the gospel." There are real sufferings to be endured for the gospel, and a theology of suffering is something sadly lacking in the Western church. The Sri Lankan writer Ajith Fernando, in his booklet titled *An Authentic Servant*, says:

> Christians from affluent countries may be losing their
> ability to live with inconvenience, stress and hard-
> ship, as there is more and more emphasis on comfort

and convenience. Many are unable to stick to their commitments when the going gets tough. They leave their places of service, change churches, and discard their friends. Some discard their spouses far too soon when their marriage faces problems. What will this mean for the church in the West? Might the West soon disqualify itself from being a missionary-sending region?

That is a big question for the church to answer and one that cannot be addressed in a book of this nature. We do want to acknowledge the suffering that is endured for the sake of the gospel by those who go to live in remote places, in conditions of want and need, in places where violence is the norm and people fear for their own safety and that of their families. Many who return home early do so because of traumatic situations that have occurred on the field. In their debriefing, they need time not just to unpack emotionally what they have seen and endured but also to grapple with the consequent spiritual questions. Equally, however, we want people to gain a proper perspective on their lives, on their shared humanity, and on those things that are part of a life lived in an increasingly mobile world. Accepting that the international community shares the stress of re-entry, the need to explore the meaning of cross-cultural transition and integrate the past with the future is a normalizing experience. It gives returnees permission to feel as they do, to affirm their identity as global nomads, and to move on, without calling their faith into question.

How can we best deal with the experience from a biblical point of view, whether we are the global nomads or whether we are the sending church, mission agency, or personal supporters?

PILGRIM'S PROGRESS

In his book *A Long Obedience*, Eugene Peterson identifies that the Bible has two designations for people of faith: *disciple* and *pilgrim*.[2] As disciples (*mathetes* is the Greek word), we are apprenticed to our master, Jesus Christ, in a growing-learning relationship at the workshop of a craftsman. As a pilgrim (*parepidemos* is the Greek word), we are people who spend our lives going somewhere—*to* God, *by* the way of Jesus Christ.

Pilgrims are people on a journey with a purpose; they have a place of departure and a place of arrival. It is a biblical image that we have lost, partly because fewer people go on pilgrimages now and partly because pilgrimages became discredited when they were associated with gaining merit, self-flagellation, and seeking a mediator other than Jesus. But the Bible is rich in images of pilgrimage.

We are a people in transition. We have been called out, like Abraham, and are on our way to "the city with foundations, whose architect and builder is God" (Hebrews 11:10). The image of pilgrimage is particularly apposite for the cross-cultural community, most of whom live with their suitcases mentally packed. The New Testament idea of us living in tents (2 Corinthians 5:1) and the impermanence of this life has been stifled in many of our home communities by the desire to cling to possessions, places, and people. We have lost the ability to live by faith as Hebrews 11:13 says: "All these people were still living by faith when they died. They did not receive the things promised; they only saw them and welcomed them from a distance. And they admitted that they were aliens and strangers on earth."

The words "alien" and "stranger" occurred frequently in my research for this book. They are concepts the mobile missions community readily identifies with. Discovering a biblical identity, pattern, or precedent for your experience helps to make sense of it in the framework of the master plan being worked out by God.

Psalms 120–134 are the "Psalms of Ascents," sung by the pilgrims on their way to Jerusalem. Eugene Peterson said that these psalms are songs of transition that provide courage, support, and inner direction for getting us to where God is leading us in Jesus Christ.[3]

William Faulkner, quoted in the program notes of the Baltimore Symphony Concert, May 5, 1977, said: "They are not monuments, but footprints. A monument only says, 'At least I got this far,' while a footprint says, 'This is where I was when I moved on again.'"

Discovering our identity as pilgrims helps us accept the loss of all that was precious to us in the previous location. It acknowledges that those people and places were significant to us and that they will not cease to be part of our journey and experience. But it also allows us to look forward to the next staging post and face the impermanence of the future, safe in the knowledge that there is an enduring goal.

Moreover, as Christians, we rest in the knowledge of an unchanging God, no matter how much our circumstances, our roles, and our conditions in life may change. Many Scriptures speak of God's unchanging nature:

- Every good and perfect gift is from above, coming down from the Father of the heavenly lights, who does not change like shifting shadows. (James 1:17)

- I the LORD do not change. (Malachi 3:6)

- Know therefore that the LORD your God is God; he is the faithful God keeping his covenant of love to a thousand generations of those who love him and keep his commands. (Deuteronomy 7:9)

Psalm 84:5–8 is a description of the blessings of pilgrimage. It speaks of those who have "set their hearts on pilgrimage." To regard ourselves as a transient people is a decision we have to make, whether we go overseas or remain in our passport countries. This Psalm speaks of the blessings that pilgrims receive, the "autumn rains" in the Valley of Baca ("dryness"). This speaks of refreshment that comes down from above. God meets us in the dry and desert places.

And pilgrims are also able to bless others in the desert. They "make it a place of springs" while on their pilgrimage. Springs are where other people and animals come and find refreshment. It is often out of our desert experiences that God speaks to us, and we find we have something to offer others.

These pilgrims, like those of Chaucer, travel in a group; they go together. We are not designed to do pilgrimage on our own. Western values, in particular, stress independence rather than interdependence. God gives his pilgrims enough strength for each day, each phase of their pilgrimage: "They go from strength to strength." But also they go at their own pace and arrive at their appointed times: "Till each appears before God in Zion." We are not here to compare ourselves with others but to support each other in our pilgrimage, wherever that may take us. Even in the desert, the valley of Baca, God has purposes for us.

The Israelites were a pilgrim people when they were on the Exodus march. They traveled in the wilderness to get to the Promised Land. They had much to discover about themselves and about their God and his purposes.

TCKS IN THE BIBLE

For Third Culture Kids who deal with similar issues of identity and transition and question where their faith fits in, a study of some of the TCKs of the Bible is helpful. TCKs in the Bible? Yes, there are several, if you stop to give it some thought. Consider the following:

- **Moses.** Brought up in a foreign culture with foster parents, he demonstrated a confusion of identity— who was he and where did he really belong? To the Egyptians he was a Hebrew, and to the Hebrews he was an Egyptian. Ultimately, he discovered that his upbringing and cross-cultural experiences were perfect for the role God had planned for him as the leader of an itinerant people.

- **Joseph.** In his early life Joseph was made to feel very special, and then his life was turned upside down. Transported to Egypt against his wishes from his home environment, he plumbed the depths of despair. However, he learned that God can bring good out of bad and his timing is perfect. When Joseph's brothers came to Egypt, he was forced to revisit the traumatic events of his life. Finally, he was able to integrate the experience into his life history and effect reconciliation within his family.

- **Ruth.** She left her home and her people and committed herself to a new loyalty. Ruth was ready to move at a moment's notice and learned that bad things happen to good people. She had the choice of being bitter or of moving on. She chose to surrender to God's will for her life and discovered that "in all things God works for the good of those who love him" (Romans 8:28).

- **Esther.** She could have asked the question, Why me? Part of a cultural minority in an alien land with strange customs, politics, and religion, at the whim of an autocratic ruler and with only an uncle to guide her, Esther was placed in a position where she could exert incredible influence but at great personal cost. She held to the values of her faith and community and took the opportunity, facing its attendant risks. She discovered the truth of being born "for such a time as this" (Esther 4:14) and the fact that God was working out his purposes.

- **Daniel.** He was moved from his home country during his student years and became the model international student. Daniel dared to be different, living out the courage of his convictions in an alien environment; he accepted the challenges and situations presented to him without compromising his faith. He drew

strength from a close personal relationship with his
God and refused to live in the past and what might
have been or to resent what had been done to him.
He lived in the present and planned positively for the
future.

Some missionary kids keenly feel the weight placed on their
shoulders to be "the perfect kid." Sometimes this is because their
parents place high and unrealistic expectations on their performances, and sometimes it is because the success of their parents'
ministry is measured in terms of the achievements and lifestyles
of the children. One MK from a traditional mission background
said: "Guilt is associated with knowing we could ruin our parents'
career. As an MK you may have had to do your little dog-'n-pony
show for the church. You had to be the perfect child or your parents might not get their support. So we deny those normal human
emotions and stuff them deep down inside."

Still others feel they are just part of the baggage their parents carry around and that sending agencies and churches do not
pay sufficient attention to their needs when arranging postings or
home assignments. One who returned from an isolated mission
outpost put it like this:

It still angers me that I hear so much church talk
about missionaries seeking to save the lost and so
little about their own children. Many mission organizations these days take much more care for their
youngest, most innocent members, but there still
exists within the church this overall lack of regard.
When I try to explain it to the folks back home, their

eyes glaze over and they soon seem to tire of the
subject. Tales of emotional adjustment are not nearly
as exciting as those about angels protecting missionaries in the jungle or heathen converts burning idols.
Lost MK souls don't seem to count as much as lost
souls in faraway lands.

Returning MKs may themselves be on a journey of faith in
which they have not yet arrived at a point of conviction. Some
have been damaged by the ministry. It is important for senders
and parents to accept them unconditionally and to support them
through this journey. The majority of MKs with whom I work
affirm their experiences in positive terms without denying the
pain that has been involved in multiple farewells. Churches and
supporters can be sensitive to their feelings by not putting them
on parade every time they come home or expecting them to be
super-spiritual.

The following advice came from a group of returning MKs:

- "Don't treat me like a celebrity; just let me be
  normal."
- "Pursue me as a friend, quickly."
- "Let me watch for a while before expecting me to
  participate."
- "Let me be a kid; don't expect me to be super-
  spiritual."
- "Pray for me."
- "Show me around the church and take me to youth
  activities."

- "Help me to fit in by telling me about music and fashions."

- "Introduce me to your friends."

THE "PEDESTAL" MENTALITY

"My greatest frustration upon return was people's expectations of a retired missionary."

"There was a deep sense of being out of control and driven by circumstances and the question of the moral rightness of leaving when national colleagues could not."

"The frustration lay in not knowing why God had not healed me and leaving the place we felt we were meant to be."

"There was spiritual confusion and loss of confidence. I felt out of kilter."

The first comment expresses the frustration of most returning cross-cultural workers—what I call the "pedestal" mentality. Churches put their missionaries on a pedestal and consequently have high expectations of them. They are the supersaints who have been "called" to the "field." Some of this is the result of a deficient theology that fails to see that all Christians have a vocation and need to be serving where God has called them.

Some expressed the frustration of returning to home-based ministries only to be considered second-class citizens:

"We had to deal with a change of ministry and the perception of others that we were no longer 'real' missionaries."

"Some individuals were wonderful, but the church policy was unsympathetic to our new home-based ministry."

I once came across this definition of a missionary: "A missionary is an ordinary person serving an extraordinary God." The comments at the beginning of this section express the reality of the situation. Cross-cultural workers are human beings with the same weaknesses, vulnerabilities, temptations, and fears as the rest of us. They fail and they fall. They experience disappointment and fail to live up to expectations. The sad thing is that expectations of them are very high, and so they have much further to fall. Most missionaries find it hard to be totally honest about their experiences and feelings while overseas, for fear of the fall-out from such revelations. They need to be given permission to be sinners as well as saints. Churches need to temper their expectations with realism.

I encourage missionaries to have a small, intimate support group while they are overseas, people with whom they can be completely honest. This is a group that will not condemn them for expressing doubts, feeling overwhelmed, sinning, and harboring negative emotions. If you can bring yourself to be totally open and vulnerable with a trustworthy group, then the prayer that is made for you will be informed and precise.

Debriefing is an important part of accepting who you are and of validating your experience. One returnee, after multiple assignments in remote areas of Africa, wrote:

I think that mission leadership should make it a
point to debrief returning missionaries, giving them
time and asking leading questions to help them
express the feelings and process the experiences they
have had on the field. If there have been difficult
circumstances leading up to their decision to leave,
the returnees are not likely to feel free to share all
that they've gone through, unless the situation is appropriate and ample, leisure time is provided, and the
interviewer shows genuine concern and interest.

Another person, returning from a long period of service in
India, affirmed how helpful such a debriefing had been:

The organization that I worked with gave me a final
appraisal of my work and time in the country. I think
this helped in closing my time there. My regional
rep also interviewed me about how I was feeling,
which was supportive. On my Home Assignment,
the year prior to my returning, I also had a chance to
talk through my work, sharing my frustrations and
thoughts for the future with the committee. They were
very helpful, and this led to me planning to return to
the field for only nine months. This gave me time to
bring closure and to think positively about my future.

Churches also need to beware of making the assumption that
the returnee is either glad to be home or finds the home church
better than the national church.

"Leaving a very lively Brazilian church to come back
to a traditional one was tough. Churches need to be

taught that their missionaries will change and, yes, *miss* being abroad. So many think we're only too pleased to be able to return to all the comforts, but we're often not."

"In France the church is very obviously struggling for its existence. Here it seems to be thriving, but may be often unaware of the real needs elsewhere. This gives us the feeling that people here are short-sighted and monocultural, and it is one of the biggest frustrations to fitting in."

Those who most appreciated the reception they received from mission leadership, churches, and supporters said the following:

- "It helped to be part of a fellowship where we were not expected to be the ones providing resources, care, and advice."
- "There needs to be someone in the mission with the authority to give you directions and also permission not to have to rush into things."
- "My church gave me six months off."
- "Friends in the church helped us to find a house and get schooling sorted out."
- "I enjoyed fellowship with my local church, and being allowed to just *be* helped me enormously."
- "I valued very much being treated as a real person rather than as 'our missionary who has come home.'"
- "People really listened."

Being part of a community of faith means mutual responsibility and mutual accountability. If missionaries expect the home church to understand their feelings, missionaries need to do the same themselves. They need to stand in the shoes of the receiving body and ask themselves, "What must it be like for them?" This person who has been a distant part of the fellowship for some time now appears resurrected before them. How can the church begin to understand what it has been like for you? Before you rush into judgment, take time to evaluate your experiences and expectations. If the church has high expectations of you, maybe your expectations of the church are also too high.

Mutual responsibility also includes communicating and rebuilding the relationship. Those who have kept in close contact while away and received periodic visits from home fared best. Upon return, both parties have to take the initiative in rebuilding the relationship and establishing understanding. One missionary returning from working on Bible translation commented: "We found that a number of people were used to *us* coming home and taking responsibility to do all the contacting. It has been interesting to see how friendships, when you are permanently here, can only work when both sides take the initiative."

MOVING ON

The Bible has many examples of people for whom telling their stories and receiving practical care were important ingredients in moving on.

- When Joseph encountered his brothers, he gave them space to tell their stories and express their feelings of distress and anger. This led to reconciliation and mutual acceptance. (Genesis 44–45)

- When Elijah was fearful, exhausted, and fleeing from Ahab, the first thing God provided for him was food and sleep. Only when his physical needs were met did God begin to address his other problem. Elijah was twice given the opportunity to tell his story. Then God was able to move him on to think about the future and the support he would receive in the form of other believers and a co-worker in the person of Elisha. (1 Kings 19)

- In his despair at the state of the ruined city and the plight of his people, Nehemiah was given time by the king to speak about his plans. He was then given the help he needed to move forward. (Nehemiah 1)

- The woman who had been bleeding for twelve years was invited by Jesus to come forward to tell her story so that she could receive not just physical healing but also emotional healing. The public acknowledgement of her plight allowed Jesus to restore her to society. (Luke 8)

- On the road to Emmaus, the traumatized disciples were met by Jesus, but they did not recognize him. He invited them to tell him everything that had happened and how they felt about it. Jesus helped them put their feelings and experiences into a new perspective. (Luke 24)

The Bible also acknowledges the rightness of expressing feelings, whether negative or positive, as a part of moving on. The psalms of David are full of righteous indignation, of pain and perplexity, of loneliness and abandonment, and of questions and remonstrations. Job was given permission to present his case before God and voice his hurt and disappointment. Neither Job nor David was condemned by God. Part of the healing and resolution process is the ability to express negative thoughts without fear of being condemned.

The Bible also speaks of the need to move on, of not clinging to the past but seeing God "doing a new thing" (Isaiah 43:18–19). Scripture promises that God has plans for our lives, plans for a "hope and a future" (Jeremiah 29:11). It speaks of seasons in our lives, seasons for everything, "a time to weep and a time to laugh, a time to mourn and a time to dance" (Ecclesiastes 3:4). Jesus said to his disciples: "Now is your time of grief, but I will see you again and you will rejoice, and no one will take away your joy" (John 16:22). He also spoke of the role of creative suffering: "Unless a kernel of wheat falls to the ground and dies, it remains only a single seed. But if it dies, it produces many seeds. The man who loves his life will lose it, while the man who hates his life in this world will keep it for eternal life" (John 12:24–25).

Jesus himself was, of course, a pilgrim, a man with an itinerant ministry who had "no place to lay his head" (Matthew 8:20). He was constantly traveling, yet he allowed himself to develop friendships, deep friendships, knowing all the time the price he would pay in terms of goodbyes. When Jesus spent forty days in the desert, he was saying goodbye to Nazareth, his place of security for the first thirty years of his life. He took time to say his goodbyes to his closest friends, spending his last days with them explaining what was happening, what sort of people he wanted them to become, and how he would maintain communication and relationship with them.

Jesus is the person who came for the ultimate cross-cultural experience. As in so many things, he is the one who shares our humanity, who sympathizes with our weaknesses, and who has been tempted in every way just as we are, yet without sin. He is there at the throne of grace interceding for us, and he is able to give us mercy and grace to help us in our time of need (Hebrews 4:15–16). As Joseph Kim has said: "Every culture in the world is foreign to someone. At first it's scary, then maddening. To survive you have to grab it, fall in love with it and make it yours. God understands. He did it too."[4]

In her book *Praying Our Goodbyes*, Joyce Rupp wrote the following prayer:[5]

> *I give you praise, God of my journey,*
> For the power of love, the discovery of friends,
>   the truth of beauty,
> For the wonder of growth, the kindling of fidelity,
>   the taste of transformation,
> For the miracle of life, the seed of my soul, the
>   gift of becoming,
> For the taste of the little dyings which have
>   strengthened me for this moment,
> For the mystery of journey, the bends in the road,
>   the pauses that refresh,
> For the faith that lies deep enough to permeate
>   discouragement and anxiety.

I give you thanks, God of my journey,
For all that I have learned from the life of Jesus
   of how to say goodbye,
For those who have always stood near me and
   given me spiritual energy,
For your strength on which I can lean and your
   grace by which I can grow,
For the desire to continue on, for believing that
   your power works through me,
For being able to love so deeply, so tenderly, so
   truly,
For feeling my poorness, my emptiness, my
   powerlessness,
For believing that you will care for me in my
   vulnerability.

I ask forgiveness, God of my journey
For holding on too tightly,
For refusing to be open to new life,
For fighting off the dying that's essential for
   growing,
For insisting that I must be secure and serene,
For ignoring your voice when you urged me to let
   go,
For taking in all the goodness but being reluctant
   to share it,
For doubting my inner beauty,
For resisting the truth of my journey home to you.

I beg assistance, God of my journey,
To accept that all of life is only on loan to me,

To believe beyond this moment,
To accept your courage when mine fails,
To recognize the pilgrim part of my heart,
To hold all of life in open hands,
To treasure all that is gift and blessing,
To look at the painful parts of my life and to grow
   through them,
To allow your love to embrace me in the empty
   and lonely days,
To receive the truth of your presence,
To trust in the place of "forever hello."

NOTES

Chapter 1: Re-Entry: What Is It?

1. Philip Bock, ed., *Culture Shock: A Reader in Modern Cultural Anthropology* (NY: Alfred Knopf, 1970).

2. John Cox, "Handbook for Overseas Doctors" (occasional paper 49, Royal College of Psychiatry, London, July 2000): 22. This paper can be purchased from www.rcpsych.ac.uk/publications/.

3. David Pollock and Ruth Van Reken, *Third Culture Kids: The Experience of Growing Up Among Worlds* (Yarmouth, ME: Intercultural Press, 1999), 61–71.

4. T. S. Eliot, "Little Gidding V," *Four Quartets* (London: Faber & Faber, 1979), 47.

5. The Talmud is a collection of books and commentaries compiled by Jewish rabbis from AD 250–500, as they sought to understand the meaning of God's word for their particular situation. The Hebrew word *talmud* means "study" or "learning."

Chapter 2: Re-Entry Stress

1. Kalvero Oberg, "Culture Shock: Adjustment to New Cultural Environments," *Practical Anthropology* 7 (1960): 177–183.

2. This was stated in a personal conversation with Marjory Foyle, author of *Honourably Wounded 2nd edition* (Oxford: Monarch books, 2001 or Grand Rapids, MI: Kregel Publications, 2001).

3. Joan Rivers, *Still Talking* (NY: Random House, 1991), 169.

4. Paul Tournier, *A Place for You: Psychology and Religion* (Harper and Row, 1968), 164.

Chapter 3: Preparing to Re-enter

1. Pollock, *Third Culture Kids*, 200.

Chapter 5: Debriefing

1. Debbie Lovell-Hawker, "Debriefing after Traumatic Incidents and at the End of Assignments," *Doing Member Care Well: Perspectives and Practices from Around the World*, ed. Kelly O'Donnell (Pasadena, CA: William Carey Library, 2002). In this article the author charts a path through the process of debriefing.

2. People in Aid website: www.peopleinaid.org.

3. Polly Chan, "MK Education and Care: Lessons from Asia," *Doing Member Care Well: Perspectives and Practices from Around the World*, ed. Kelly O'Donnell (Pasadena, CA: William Carey Library, 2002), 65.

4. Richard W. Bagge, "Traumatic Stress and Families" (paper presented at a training seminar, 1999): 4.

Chapter 6: Who Am I?

1. Nik Baker and Daida Moreno, *The Ultimate Guide to Windsurfing* (London: Harper Collins, 2001), 14.

2. Ruth Hill Useem, "Third Culture Kids: Focus of Major Study," *Newslinks* 12, no. 3 (January 1993): 1. (Newspaper of the International School Services)

3. Pollock, *Third Culture Kids*; Marion Knell, *Families on the Move* (London: Monarch Books, 2001).

4. Ruth Goring Stewart, "I am Green," *MTI/Children's Intercultural Program: DAR Breakthrough*, 66.

5. Miriam Dyer, "Belonging," *Interact Magazine* (2001). *Interact* is a magazine that discusses important issues in MK/TCK education and care. For more information see the website: http://www. tckinteract.net/interact/overview.htm.

Chapter 7: The Emotional Roller Coaster

1. E.T. Cook and A. Wedderburn, eds., *John Ruskin Works* (London: George Allen, 1903–12), 36:125–6; letter to his father dated January 28, 1852.

2. Maxine Waters was quoted in Brian Lanker, *I Dream a World: Portraits of Black Women Who Changed America* (NY: Stewart, Tabori & Chang, 1989).

Chapter 8: Nuts and Bolts

1. Cas Clarke, *The Essential Student Cookbook: 400 Budget Recipes to Leave Home With* (Headline Publishing, 2002); Jean Patterson and Danae Campbell, *Cooking Outside the Pizza Box: Easy Recipes for Today's College Student* (Barron's Educational Series, 2004).

Chapter 9: The Third Culture Community

1. T. S. Eliot, "The Dry Salvages," *Four Quartets* (London: Faber & Faber, 1979), 34.

Chapter 10: The Reception Committee

1. Joyce Rupp, *Praying our Goodbyes* (Eagle Publishing, 2002), 21–22.

Chapter 11: The Pilgrim Community

1. Friedrich Nietzsche, *Beyond Good and Evil*, trans. Helen Zimmern (London, 1907), sec. 188.

2. Eugene Peterson, *A Long Obedience in the Same Direction: Discipleship in an Instant Society* (Downers Grove, IL: InterVarsity Press, 2000), 17.

3. Ibid., 20.

4. Joseph Kim, "Parenting and Educating TCKs Well," *Interact Magazine*, (December 2000).

5. Joyce Rupp, *Praying our Goodbyes*, 122–123.